Purification of Divine

Transformation of Barbarism to Almighty

USHA PARAKH

BLUEROSE PUBLISHERS
India | U.K.

Copyright © Usha Parakh 2023

All rights reserved by author. No part of this publication may be reproduced, stored in a retrieval system or transmitted in any form or by any means, electronic, mechanical, photocopying, recording or otherwise, without the prior permission of the author. Although every precaution has been taken to verify the accuracy of the information contained herein, the publisher assumes no responsibility for any errors or omissions. No liability is assumed for damages that may result from the use of information contained within.

BlueRose Publishers takes no responsibility for any damages, losses, or liabilities that may arise from the use or misuse of the information, products, or services provided in this publication.

For permissions requests or inquiries regarding this publication, please contact:

BLUEROSE PUBLISHERS
www.BlueRoseONE.com
info@bluerosepublishers.com
+91 8882 898 898
+4407342408967

ISBN: 978-93-5819-720-4

Cover design: Muskan Sachdeva
Typesetting: Rohit

First Edition: November 2023

I received third eye in 2011, fourth eyes in 2017, 1st swarup of 'Mahamriteswari ' as Aalok Ghutna in 2021 and innumerable eyes in 2023.

Let human trust that God Incarnates to cleanses the world with good deeds, spiritualities, religious tolerance and tranquility. I am one of them.

I have also enrolled in Bravo international world record that I have the ability to transform the nature and correct universal time whenever I want.

 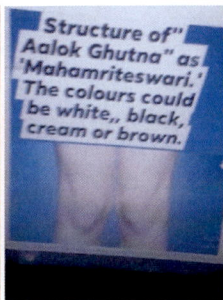 

Purification Of Divine

The world, full of artistic appearance containing awesome scenes and sceneries with innocent floras and faunas with chilled pure, fragrance of water and air when combines with pearly fountain, even the tough, rigid mountains overwhelm with joy and almighty itself astonish by its dazzling beauty, isn't it?

Stay tuned, before moving your any step forward, it has numerous realities to say and we just to listen and chew its real facts and figures to recognize this world.

The facets of a coin: head and tail imparts the derivative plan of creative human potentials that goes hand in hand with absolute power of skilled mechanism. However, negative thoughts, mental traumas, psychological tortures, inequality vanishes the real persona of well beings.

The acts and deeds of human itself lead him to the position of divine and devil. The pure form of conscience, the soul and physical outlook cherishes and enhances inner persona of well-beings that rotates the circle of love, goodness, kindness, honesty and groove the world into splendid scenario.

Moreover, negligence, harshness, backstabs chuck the man into melancholic atmosphere where crime, murder, dishonor, terrorism and hat rate explodes. So, evaluation of persona verves absolute thoughts in well-beings.

After all, if we grow cactus, rose won't bloom out from that vary plant. The genes of divine will shed the universe with the fruits of love and brotherhood and vice-versa.

From As azoic era to Paleozoic era, the war between blood sucker vampire to blood donor angels are in terms to conquer the heart and brain of animals (especially social animals). The game of defeat and victory sandwiched between the mental behavior and physical actions. The labyrinths of divine to overcome from devils are struggling hard to break them but the power-booster packs of solders are exhausted yet fighting to spread love in the universe. What a paradox!

Where's the sweetness of Adam-Eve' love that had to over last till the world turns to paradise... Where the footsteps of Mahatma Gandhi, Mother Teresa hat are has viewed the path of tranquility and prosperity? Where's the colorful, aromatic garden of Lord Krishna where he funk with gopiyaas? Are they buried under the symmetry of selfish world or we, human are blind to see those divinity power.

Sun's Bacon has motto, to spread light in the whole universe. However, it falls in prism, it scatters numerous hues. Likewise, God message is to save humanity. However, it falls on world and scatters in the form of Hinduism, Muslims, Christians, Jainism and Buddhism. Moreover, the intention of the message is same.

Envious nature, Shady behavior, Caste discriminations, inequality are the true devils that are sucking the world into physical success. In opposition, philanthropy organizations, Charity, mankinds are the real seraphs that splits glimpse of humanity.

The seraphs are always greeted for cozy wishes in the castle of heart as they're boon for universe .Devils are thrashed yet conceived the mind of today's generation. Smuggling, human trafficking, rave party have seized the minds of today's generations just for the physical pleasure whose fruits could be pretty poisonous.

Now, the world is in the form of Apple-Extract wine. The addition of comfort game has chucked the world into suffocation yet sophistication zone. Oh no! Peace is my way, divine whispers

The breathing process that we inhale (Oxygen) and exhale (carbondioxide) is stacked with divine and devil methodologies. When we consume oxygen, pure, fresh air enters in our body, new cell membrane emerges when we exhale carbon dioxide, and we throw unwanted harmful gases from our body. So, the whole system of body is influenced by peace and anger postures.

The spiritual energy that showers blessings, purity, happiness, absolute power who converts dream into action with miraculous willpower is the real serenity on Earth whose jest is to spread love and harmony in each and every creature to rectify the wrong deeds of human who has lost himself into the world of pain, agony and worry.

Verbal diarrhea, allegations are the communicable disease that has swallowed the universe. The Dracula in the human form has burned the world with negative atomic energy. Violence, ego, jealousy, crab-mentality has murdered the soul and conscience who are pleasing the outer shell of soul. "Alas! Body isn't in my control" soul screams…

Purification of Divine

Meditation, yoga, motivational songs, soothing music relaxes the brain and rejuvenates energy to evoke the conscience again. Love is the best panacea for all the disease. Spread love to get love .This is the most powerful method to abolish culture of agony and hatred.

The twinkling stars of the moon scatters the silvery light with the message of peace .The calm nature can absorb all the worries and problems .Smile in the face and love in the eyes can hypnotize any creatures to live in paradise-with prosperity in the closet of globe. Lovely, directors are now soft-hearted to inculcate hard work in the actors.

The solar system has a family where king (sun) enlightens all the planet .They revolve around the sun and have definite parameters. The planets perform their tasks at their best. They all possess absolute powers who maintain their lifestyles easy and longest, the livelier you are, the more lifespan you can achieve. Cheerful life is the key to success.

The sarcastic behavior invites negative horrible energy who only just not destroys the relations of human. They just not destroy the relations of human but also create vampire in the body of human. That's why; almighty generates great spirits to remove dark shadow of manipulative dreary demon.

In reality, our body is made up of infinite atoms and molecules particles. Positive atoms when increase in our body, happiness, success, longevity raises more and more .That's why, childhood is the most pleasing stage of life. However, different stages of life teach lesions in the selfish world. So, when we, reach in the old stage, agony attacks and negative atoms increases which is the ultimate reason why people scares to enter in the elderly stage.

Earth is a beautiful planet. Breathtaking natural beauties, icy-cool Mountains, Silvery Mountain with the golden touch of Sun, aromatic colorful buds who romance with naughty butterflies, animals; proud of jungles and we, humans have naughty, chocolaty nature that blends with everyone to make the Earth worthiest in the Solar family .Aren't we; the shiny stars of Earth, yes, we are.

The fragrance of the world clashes in the terms of Racism, ego, equality, color, divorce filling, and misunderstanding has spread its powerful wings. The body of greed is snatching the superficial souls to convert them to dangerous dragon. The inner conscience is somehow breaking the shackles of devils to spread light of freedom, happiness, and creating the way of noble destiny.

When we take sun bask, light enters throughout the spores of our body, who dazzles to eradicate dark devils who control the brain to perform mischievous deeds. After all ,the biggest almighty is nature and atmosphere .

Each and every activity we perform is visible by our soul .Good deeds leads to happiness, pleasure, prosperity and longevity whereas, chit grips into the way of hell where agony suffering, hat rate juggles with life of fool creatures.

The silvery dew when fall into green grasses. The calm nature forgets about global issues .They just enjoys and has fun with their loved ones. And we, human regret small matter to destroy our living standard. Only few spirits grow and groom in the contradictory circumstances to make Earth a better place than heaven.

We, human have superficial abilities, hardship and super willpower to achieve anything what we want to have. We reached on Mars, we reached beneath the ocean, we fly with airy wings (jets and plane). In short, we are best creatures in the universe. But, why do we poke our nose on others matters. Why do we envy? Can we resolve issues to revive happiness in life? Actually, there is some genuine person who believes in action, determination, dedication, passion to make the world go speechless. Then how's the problem arises?

Purification of Divine

'I' is the term of all the issues. We hesitate to rely on others. Somehow, tapestry of 'Ecosystem' is disturbed due to 'Ego system' (Only 'I').

Ups and down is the phenomenon of life. Over Excitement and Depression both are slow poisons for life. Balanced life-cycle should be maintained to tackle the problems and handle the excitements. Only 10% of our brain is utilized by Human. Nicole Barr, Albert Aaistain, Steve Hawkins's brain worked more than 13% which is exceptional. Jealousy, frustration, anger, stress occupy more attention of brain because of which we lose our capability, Visualization and keep our self in paralysis world.

Get Up, grow Up, We can think better, work harder. Remember we are 'Human', not 'Humor 'best creature of world. Dignity, self-respect and love are the prime needs from which we can lead or direct into the way of glory and tranquility.

Harmony, mutual understanding can groove the mesmerizing world into the direction of progress, opportunity and progress. Whenever we are contained, Success automatically revitalizes the life happiness. So, absolute, positive nature is the greatest source to achieve success and happiness in life.

Cyclone, hurricane, landslide are the synonyms of destruction. It comes rapidly and destroys everything, so does anger and frustration. When it attacks, it absorbs divinity power and disturbs health .Therefore, calm peace nature showers tranquility and prosperity in life.

Generosity, Compassion, blessings are the key methodologies to synthesize love and jolliness. This amends agony to amenities and purifies the soul. Helping nature is so far the worthiest essence for cheerful life. Honesty plays the crucial role to fill the heart with sweet, soft feelings.

The value of Esperit-de-corps is incredible. World fragmentation just spread agony and hat rate in the heart of people .Therefore, it's better to unite the states, unite the people so that we can entitle the Earth as' united universe'-enlightening absolute energy to ignite icons. Oh! My Kasha…my eyes and my heart depicts the beautiful reverie .I'm sure, this is going to be true someday.

When people understand the importance of love, liberty, equality, no doubt, we help to popularize our universe as best planet of solar system.

The high range of mountain signifies that they will always stand for their dignity and aim high .No matter, how catastrophic circumstances it handles with patience. Natural disasters like Earthquake, flood occurs but they afraid to move rock solid mountains. So should be the human performance. When the wings of creativity are focused to fly in the sky of ambition, it should reach to its destiny .No, silly excuses are needed to control or stop their ambition.

The continuous waves of sea, the gradual growth of living creature's showcase that good karma should be performed continuously. It's the topmost priority of human beings, because we human are born for the sake of humanity, for the welfare of world.

Snake bite is pretty dangerous .It's poisionous can chuck the person into the demise stage. But Scientists found that snake'poision contains some medical properties too, which has the ability to cure chronic and major diseases. Venom is not just the life donor but it also the panacea to cure nervous system disease, cancer, destroys tumor cells, aids to overcome from Parkinson and even heart attacks, crashes blood pressure problems and collapse the hazards of strokes. Researchers also proclaims that toxins when develops into drugs, dramatizes the dreadful disease to have distinct, dynamic and life to dazzle the world from distinguish actions.

So does human spirits. Wrong deeds lead you to the world of pain and sufferings and good deeds always cure and heal the aspirations to shatter the shackles of limits and cuddles with infinity.

Our aspirations, desires, thinking process denotes the quality we posses, good company cultivates positive atmosphere, absolute attitude and inculcate sophistication in life styles. So, positive vibes supports and uplifts creativity and drag you into the field of humanity.

Great eminent Scholars are grown and brought-up in positive atmosphere so that they can bring revolutions in the ill-mannered society. Their education, their ability can evoke the world to stand for their rights and conquer creative cosmos to croon with distinct collaborations. They are the pure divine souls born to eradicate the evil spirits of the society and grab tremendous achievement to enroll the exotic world dazzled, desperate and simply out of the world.

Purification of Divine

From my Opinion, Education is exceptionally powerful to uplift and transform the society. Education brings awareness in a person that gives sensibility to perform right job to amalgamation of corruption and conspiracy. That also depicts Cultivation of culture and manner in which environment you're brought-up and grown-up. So, education plays a crucial role to move people in the direction of dignity, self –esteem and self-achievement.

I think trees are the loveliest creatures on Earth .They are born to give life to others. They're the synonyms of patience whose great deeds are lascivious for others creatures too especially who are nurtured under their shadows ,embarked in the shell or the visitors to have something nutritious.

The lesson of dawn and dusk preaches once you're born, be a successor to achieve exceptional victory. Reach the apex of happiness and fulfill thy ambition before leaving the Earth .When you are self-contained, you definitely goanna rock the paradise entitling 'Earth'.

Three portions of Earth are covered with aqua and a solo portion is with land. More than eight billion populations with other terrestrial creatures stay together for the functions of smooth eco-system .By utilizing single portions of land by terrestrial beings, globe has signified the importance of water … Think, if water is used with conservation, we can utilize and acquire more precious resources from hydra's community. Today's generation and future generation will secure gems of genuine commodity along with get the spell of cushy curtsy who are doctrine as mermaid , blesses and bliss to drive the life with diligence and decency in order to achieve success with passionate performance.

'Masiha 'is the life-donor term. He/she generally fulfils the wishes and desires of living-beings. We all humans are Masiha from our spirits, who come to concrete the culture and civilization of humanity. Genuinely, Devine power in the soul shells (human body) definitely empowers not only the people but also to the whole universe.

Jokes part, Devine and devilry power adds spices and seasoning flavors' in our life. It examines our inner strength and caters stamina to leave no stone unturned. It boosts to remove hurdles of our life. Though these powers are utterly paradox to each-others, that makes the human better ever.

The chest nut, walnuts, ground nuts has very hard outer shell but contains very worthy fruits inside. So, should be the human. No matter how you look, how rock solid you're by nature but should be very smoothie ,soft –hearted and have very good feelings and compassion for the needy one. Yes…, yes…,yes… now, humanity in our way!

Socialization, communication with people, group conversations are some of the major tools that helps in connecting people and share their suppression and excitement feelings with one-another .It encourages some individuals to involve themselves in social warfare zone which not only upgrade the social status but also encourages and allows other persons to participate for other cause.

The sensibility, courage and intent of life drag the lines of awareness .It awakens people, motivate them and lead to the path of success and good actions. Divinity power helps in uplifting the culture, the high morale and boosts the vibrant energy in well-beings.

Our heart is a pure heritage where God stays and transform us as pure divine. Creatures add spark and enlighten in the universe whereas, our brain as sometimes treats as part and portion of devil who wrongly focuses to throw mangy cards to rule the universe.

We human are real manifestation of divine that are created with the motto to exhilarate every human creature found in the world..The more positive atoms in the body the more absolute energy sustains in the inner and outer world. Therefore, we must spruce ourselves to bring revolutions in the world to entitle human as 'crème-de-la-crème' in the solar community.

To breach the stereotype practice and dogmatic beliefs and superstitions, one ought to realize what our soul conveys .The ladder of love will definitely makes you reach at the apex of spiritual power where you love to be lost in the lap of almighty.

Sometimes, the sinking behavior also drags the human into the path of felony where he considers himself as devil. He performs fraud, cheating, corruption and nasty activities to earn property and fake prosperity to recognize himself as Don, What a pity!

The glimpse of love, charm and jolliness when exuberates from inward, the outer world seem to be paradise that ceases harmful vibes and cherishes splendid personifications too.

Therefore, the strategy to embrace the mankind is to break the shackles of crabby behavior that are holding fuddy-duddy and enlightening pure soul to create sensational mentality and environment (especially for future generation) .

The optimistic mind accumulates positive cosmic energy that helps to eradicate the negative karmic layer from the soul and that can only be obtained through yoga, meditation and good karma. These things benefit the mentality and cherry-pick the positivity from the whole astronomical areas. Therefore, existence of divine power not only caters self-achievements in the person but also bring great awareness in the 'Earth'. The supernatural power beholds absolute tranquility to dive their destiny 'A castle of Glory'.

God turns as a mentor to preach mercy to dissolve negative deeds that are hampering the humanity causing endless agony .Their supersonic sound reverbertirates feeling of generosity, seeds of love and dedicate you for the philanthropy causes which scatters mutual obligations, harmony and sense of brotherhood.

The pros and cons of divine and devilry power energize and enrapture the heart, mind, body and soul of person of which makes their sustainability tedious yet adventures. The holy power when doctrines about the liberty from birth and demise that can only be achieved when you have complete control over the mind and purification of soul with dissolved karma whereas the negative power persuades the human for physical pleasure, biological needs and monitory values which entangle them to focus on tangible matters.

The rocks, submarines, woods all have distinguish features are considered to be boon and blessing of nature alive as sweet memento .Nature also showers the expected requirements to match-up human desires. These are the divinity power that is the indirect form of 'Kalpwriksh'. Therefore, evoke thy conscience to grab the positivity spread in the form of nature i.e. visible form of God.

The tapestry of ecosystem is attached with each and every living species in universe. Their chain has to be sequentially maintained so as to balance natural environment. If one species in endangered, other will zeopadise soon.Therefore,divine urges not to hamper biological environment and make anyone stable and colorful because nature laws conveys love and respect the nature and receive the same in bulk and vice-versa.

Each and every cell of the body pop-up when divine forces enchants the Vedic term to revitalize the conscience for esperit-de-corps. This helps to rejuvenate and activates the brain to follow the path of brotherhood. Hence, evil and devil minimizes when good deeds exalts.

The heart and nervous system has inseparable connections that evokes kundilini to detoxify negative energy and creating insane absolute power from the cosmos through meditation and yoga .It helps to purify the soul and advocates to dissolve sin by continuous performance of charity, good jobs and positive thinking.

Our body is composed of five elements. They are Earth, Fire, Marine and sky. These elements combines together to form human structure. These most powerful elements aids in securing supernatural power and all the aesthetic experiments that's hard nut to crack. Therefore, when heart, body, nervous system generates positive seeds of love i.e. protons- the whole solar community showers grace and blessings to acquire fine and divine power in the human.

The ego and bitchy behaviors is the most dangerous monster in human being. They evade jolliness and drag the person into hell which allows pain to shut the gate of success. This hits another dignity and self-esteem too which sometimes leads to shatter delicate relations .So, in order to commence delicate bonds in society ,one must emphasis on selfless responsibilities to magnetize himself or herself to match-up the needs and requirements of society which will help o bloom the nation someday and give pleasant fragrance to the globe .

The multimillionaire personality like Warren Buffet ,Birla Tata, Dhirubhai Ambani were not aliens but have extreme features but have extreme features to conquered the Earth with their hard toil and dedication .Their ceaseless effort and killer instinct set the world on fire which is showering the droplets of happiness to the needy one. Yes, they are also the form of divine who has incarnated to fulfill all the basic and additional needs of destitute

The world is being fragmented because of chaotic vision, misconception and lack of uniformity indecision-making process. The tendency of being superior and fishy minds always greet fragile bonds among people which leads squabble, ultimately transmits deceptions, dishonor and freezes the namby-pamby relations.

We human, the protagonists of all creatures are greatest blessings of Almighty, meant to serve humanity and has assignment to extract the greatest zeal that's keeps us restless., hunting us from inside to prove that we are incredible and nonesuch legends who landed on Earth to cater some smashing gifts to the globe.overall,the main synopsis is to inculcate euphoria in each and every heart of living creatures to let the world rocking and sizzling.

The embryos of love and compatibility germinates with miraculous seeds to adhere liberalization and to get out of narrow-minds and hypocracy.That are intact in the petals of harmony to speculate the world ,the power of seraphs and to make the world go speechless. The prime crucial agenda to revive pure energy is very much love indeed. Oh yaa! People are almost shackle free from segregated world.

Rose, a beautiful creation of nature is pampered by all. Because of it's look and fragrance , it wishes to cuddle with bees. Wow, rose's thorns are quite spiny which injures everyone who come across the plants but it sticks with the features to bloom and spread pleasant aroma all around, so should be the human. No matter how catastrophic circumstances he or she faces but should have positive attitude and behavior for the world's welfare.

The prophet propagates about the spirituality and cosmic energies that our soul comprises of. Human soul consists of transcend knowledge and ethical values which is esteemed. He /she liberalizes about the award winning programmers that he/she conducts for the upliftment and purifications of soul and to exhilarate the human conscience.

Almighty drizzles fine aura and countless blessings in each individual which accompany them to decompose the devastating effects of sin and gruesome impacts of mischievous acts .The absolute energy also advocates about the theory of 'Live and let live' . Administration of magnificent scenes and sceneries around the world and adoring scenes in inner conscience .When interact together, pure souls funk with joy. Oh! Devilry power perplexes!

Each cell contains millions and trillions of atoms which evaluates and synchronizes the human body to have flawless functions .They enclaves the aesthetics of pure source so as to remove hurdles ,produced by negativity. Although positive power and negative energy chock a block together .They allure inner strength and fighting spirit to seize victory.

The orthodox practices that slashes human heart should be abolished so that we can embrace the witty concepts to set milestones ahead .smart projections should be executed so as to meet desires and demand of humanity .yes, cosmos whispers "I am with you"...

The right aptitude and attitude with great quench to acquire the passionate desires always proves that hardship is better than fortunes .It begins with ground level to reach the topmost level with fair guidelines to achieve success and satisfactions. This provides wings to fly high in the ambitious world and converts fairy tales into reality .Yes, divine power do exist in human to realize about the supreme authority that hail and awaken self-esteem- to recognize the power within us.

God is the pioneer of planets, sun, stars, moon, asteroids all bestow themselves and become as devotees when preaches to circulate rationalization on Earth. Supreme energy doctrines about the amendments and rectifications on the major issues that the Earth faces that the divinity power can be promoted.

Earth chills when there is abundance of compassion, moral values and justice. Therefore, biological environment is created to ignite and incline the philosophy of humanity. It also proves the lesson of giving to make the heart generous and self-content.

The outrageous actions deteroites the real charm and persona of well-beings which not only vanishes tempting personality but also adversely affects the happiness, prestige and peace from within. It shakes mankind and shatters human aspirations too. So, in order to minimize and control such actions, we must set an exceptional instance to call the Earth 'an elite planet'.

God is the best astole who delegates authorities and responsibilities to every living species .He diagnosis problems and come out with best possible solutions to cater them with favors of victory. He examines and evaluates everyone's performance and the sensational performers are rewarded with incredible fame and recognitions. Prosperity and sophistication with infinite grace. That's a bizarre to obtain!

Eminent and bonefied personalities convey that geniuses are the real gems of the world. I accept the fact, but I feel generous are the true solitaires of the world .Genius bring some praising ,tempting gifts to the globe which hypnotizes everyone. Genius people denotes some extra-ordinary things which are heart touching and makes the humanity feel proud and lively forever. When both goes hand-in-hand, divinity persists.

The toxins produced in the physical body is removed by antioxidants so as to have spontaneous functions of different system prevailing in the body.Likewise,wrong doers which attacks the empire of peace and prosperity ; positive energy incarnates and emerges to defeat and dissolve them .Sometimes, they follow non-violence movement to give the world, the feeling of ecstasy.

Tender heart personalities activate the world by splashing the essence of endurance, compassion, nobility to groove the world with tour-de-force. They are the synonyms of ethereal energy who amuses the world by turning themselves as heart-throb. They devote and dedicate each cell of their body to bring divinity force in order to allure the Earth.

Heartbeat raises with pulse rate , brain cells activates more ,soul soothes with joy ,emotions overwhelm the heart and splotches roll down the eyes when human recognize about the absolute spiritual energy that he/she contains within. The endless strength evokes and awakens to preach about anthropology and also about the science beyond the science i.e. about almighty. He also suggest to give selfless service to destitute, preserving biological nature and pamper every creature who come around which gradually helps to obtain wishes and grace from them.

Wicked wishes to get stardom and kick the jovial world .It raise issues and allows jinx to overlap and shadow the fantabulas seeds of almighty .It brings isolations and riles-up the people that causes collusion of goodness ,harmony and justice. It explodes agony with suffocation. I t inculcates diplomacy and tricky behavior and harasses mellow mentality. This is dreary dearth of humanity.

We human are the masterpiece, invented by God, with immense intelligence and generous heart. We tackle the entire obstacle skillfully and tactfully, We solve brainstorming issues and puzzles to prove that we are dynamite and above all, the creative creatures of the world. So, we should pay tribute the positive force by assembling together to incline the area of harmony ,good deeds and brotherhood.

Generally, we say cradle is the first school and mother is the first teacher. But the sperm that comes from Dad is adherent and core wish of parents are-child will pursue this profession ,what he/she is good at and bla…bla…blab…Almighty extract the best possible sperm to hit the useless one in order to fulfill the extensive desires of their dearest one .Now, convey me, who is the best teacher, the mind is in the state of perplex ion, isn't it?

The clumsy mind invites prejudiced actions and suspicious interrogations on tremendous skilled successful personalities. They create state of dilllemna n witty minds and diffuse their aspirations to bring chaos and sarcastic sensibility to depress the world. They are irrational and biggest taboos for society. Their envious nature evicts peace, harmony and love who actively anticipates in hazardous, harmful contemplations. Oh no, devil exists everywhere.

In context to book brook for the perpetual peace in the planet, pleasing policies of highly literate fraternity should be encouraged and applied. Their deliverance of speech and presentations should be delighted in such an elegant manner to sprinkle exuberance and advancement that makes the world even better. They also should be given praise, remarkable designations, accolades and awards for better performance. The major grievance for the people in today's world is they easily attach their emotions on unworthy people and rely them who compel them to face blackmailing, fraud and so on. That also hampers great loss of respect, common sense and shrinks the lively heart. This leads demoralizations and enormous sufferings to humanity.

The ideology of philosophers, writers and great leaders should be implemented to bring perpetual golden dawn on Earth and to eliminate the shade of despair to refresh the world once again .Their intelligence and intellectual heart pour patriotism and fertilize the selfish dessert into mutual harmonized garden.

Some babies are born with silver spoon where some suffers from hand to mouth situations. Some spring chickens turns themselves as spoiled brats where some jot down their destiny by hardship .Their tremendous efforts and dedications creates history and teaches remarkable that upgrades the ladder of success for betterment. When good deeds exalts, devil expels from the world.

The prodigious personage like Margret Thatcher, Indira Gandhi, Benjamin Franklin, Barrack Obama traced their apotheosis model all over the world. Their spunky and influential behavior

Proved they landed on Earth to have marvelous existence. They focused and worked on people's grievance, their issues and requirements, their sustainable developments and so on. Their powerful persona enequsited and sparkled the globe that reduced heinous adversity.

Deities are determined for those who listened to their hearts, they set miracles and extreme peace and happiness who entrust their life for selfless service and deserve invocations from tender hearts. They gain trust and baptizes with beloved child of God .Their all hankerings are fulfilled gradually when they modify themselves as a living divine on Earth.

Everyone's heart speaks and understands the language of telepathy .It's a process of communication between heart, brain and different senses that activates more when there is presence of same species around. It's a pure natural phenomenon that helps to recognize other's creature's tendency. When heart is pure and have positive force, people easily connects with deity, it gives them immense pleasure, strength, focus on their objectives and forecast their fortunes. They help and teaches to dissolve negative karma and set some fibulas' miracles to achieve what he/she is likely capable of. It's easiest than thinking process. Therefore, telepathy with supreme energy is for the best methodology to generate the positivity in ourselves and get rid from the world of pain, sufferings and misery.

Reiki is a talisman for entire body that enlightens pure souls. It's the process by which each and every atom strikes the spiritual energy to evoke, to guide and to show the path of elated worlds. The seven chakras of the body where life energy is restored illuminate more to strengthen the sacred powerhouse i.e. soul. It's the advanced versions that wipe out negativity. This process accumulates and then transmits radiant energy in the well-being. It dismisses hypothetical perceptions and chaos that whatever is happening is just the wish of God rather it clarifies the concept that best thing is going to occur from now because it's the ultimate wish of God.

According to my intuition, Ayurveda is the most ancient and powerful Vedas of the world .It's a Vedic culture that induces natural healings trough biological environment i.e. herbs, roots and the like. It balances ratios between wind (vata), bile (pitta) and phlegm (kapha) compiling in the body .It's sacred knowledge to make life long and lively. The sages from ancient India explored their proposals to rejuinivate mankind, to accelerate peace and calm environment among people. This helps in healing pain causing due to depression and devilry acts. It's a kind of therapy that exuberates the state of jolliness. It preaches best thought that how sages used to live evergreen and balanced life.

Regular chants evacuate negative energies from the body and purify each atom through spiritual power. It strengthens willpower and secures divine spirits. Continuous chants as well as group chants when collaborates each individual and the whole surrounding, plays the melody of pleasure, peace; pampered and purity then proves the panacea of pain and places all possibilities.

Continuous permanent prayer helps to provoke the pure soul and permanently discard problems. This allows complacency, good faith and simplicity in individual. It gives justice to naïve personality and allows them to tolerate with people with the simplicity. It preaches to be calm and let the karma decide to jot their destiny with love and grace .This allows blessings and patience in individual that roots to purity and peace. Continuous prayer pleases pure persona and elegance their beloved with temptations.

Kayotsarga is a Jainism therapy that comforts body and lightens the soul. It eradicates pain , sufferings, agony and heals every atoms with love and purity. It makes the body even lighter than the petals of lotus. According to Jainism, it's assumed that it's so far the easiest and best therapy to avoid jinx and to greet ecstasy. It softens the body from the head to toe. It synchronizes the divinity power to feel them as about the pure soul. This process helps to feel love that is abounded everywhere. Kayotsarga amuses the core of hearts to give the perfect rhythm to balance the hormonal changes.

Penance is the process that rectifies all the negative karma to fill full priority in the person. Sages, Acharyas, monks are almost every good souls perform penance to purify themselves. In this therapy, person leaves shortage of eatable things and sometimes too. Even if they consume boiled water, they avoid drinking water after dusk. This process helps to fulfill their utmost desires. When the soul is completely crystal clear, the body converts into pure divine form .This gives heavenly feel in the person. This helps to reduce aging problems and adds more age in human. It also helps person t stay fit and smart.

Yoga is the best therapy to heal any sort of problems, especially with physical health. It helps to bring the blood in upward direction in the body that fulfils even the tremendous wishes of human that can't be easily obtained. This method makes the human feel about the value of human body that is achieved after eighty-four lacks births .yoga helps to give longer life. This also helps to have enormous wealth, fame and prosperity ,all the happiness when it's performed properly with all the good nutritious food especially milk, curd, fruits and the like. Even God performs yoga. That's why; they're called Yogeswar and Adi Yogi. We can see lots of postures of God and Goddess that are in Yoga positions. Natraj dance is also the finest yoga position that brings ecstasy and liveliness. Surya pranayam is also the good examples of good yoga postures. It brings unlimited happiness that helps to shine all the atoms of living human body, that strengthens human life and give fitness to the person who daily performs yoga.

Meditations treat the mind, body, heart and soul in the finest manner. This helps to bring closer to the nature and supreme divine forces. It plays the natural music in each cell of the body and which is dam powerful to overcome from devilry world .It makes them feel about the power of different hues. Meditation realizes them about the countless colors of almighty that's filled and sprinkled in each and every living and non-living things. This also helps in evoking kundilini and realizes about supreme energy.

Pressing hard the point of concerned region in the outer body shell especially of palm, foot and face is derived to acupressure. Generally, it's performed with wooden pen. Wooden wheel that also gives a kind of message in the body. That helps to rejuvenate positive energy and sometimes awaken kundilini to awaken what a person desires of. This helps to get rid of diseases that are hampering the person from within. It's a slick process to be physically fit and mentally sound .so, rapture the attention by presenting thyself as icon, a gracious, glamorous personality who're incarnated to love the divine force and to encourage divinity power at par. When fine needles are inserted in the skin layer, specific points to awaken lines of meridians, then this system is followed to cure physical and mental health. It's a traditional Chinese medical theory that applied to patients with pure patience. Generally, it's controversial to western medical concept. But, its result is quite good and believed to be less painful as compare to other surgeries. This complementary system aids to eradicate pain and suffering of brain and body that has arise due to deadly diseases. As this procedures uses this machinery equipments, it's safe and kind of life giving therapy to sort out problems caused due to unhealthy lifestyles.

Palpation of body is so far the best soothing therapy to eradicate any hazards , sufferings, pain. That nourishes skin, textures, clean pores and improves blood circulation. This process evokes kundilini as well as avoids negative karmic layers. This helps to improve functions of nervous systems and cures and heals agonies of life. Daily routines frustrations and full hilarious moments to surround euphoria all around. So, let's exquisite the life with eternal love ,purity to catch divine power and the supreme energy attention.

Exceeding plan may lead to devastations but when handled but when it's handled wisely, it can change the scenario of world .Threat turns to terrific treat when an artist, mind-gambler, an educational lover grips the exerted portion to spread love in the world in order to secure the crown of prestige. The dreary ditch of deception, transform to dreamy description of designated delegate whose disciples are genuine gems and the panelist who has grooved , carved and molded the sculptures to spread the message that almighty and divine forces are the most superior. They evade evil and eradicate the negative source of energy to enequisit earth from beautiful souls and shells of prodigious performers.

Naïve generally have blind faith on God and God extremely grace to such beloved devotees. The silent killer " pain "when given to pure souls or naives, God incarnates to place the world in safe zone where sages can be saved and demons are crushed and killed from the eternal love and beautiful brains .That will host the flag of truthiness spreading the message to devote time and energy to spread tranquility. But when, blood-sucker goes for gruesome acts, then God make naives, namby-pamby person to historic legend. They show power, position, potential and passion still to be considered as child of divine energy come to conquer the world with utmost dedication and loyal commitment to jot the destiny in historical world with golden letters and make the globe glorious, gracious and glamorous. Yes, divine forces are hitched with victory.

Devil powers believes in dictatorship and hate human and humanity rather they make human to slave and slave to robots who only loves them when their rules are obeyed for personal benefit. Then divine and absolute energy approaches to drizzle love, compassion , mercy and justice to make each creature feel lovely, pretty and best. Then the globe salute the divine force and their beloved kids and get the perfect graph of beautiful and powerful scenario of splendid globe. Let the entire divine force smash and sizzle the cosmos to evoke goodness all around.

Sacrificing the life for the sake of needy, destitute and beloved one, in order to cease catastrophe and cater composure. This is the best reward one can secure. Situation then reminds that love is the purest ambrosia, compassion in the best remedy, kindness and mercy is the biggest emotional features and good actions is always the qualitative medicines that eradicate evil. Ultimately, devilry power shatters beneath the ground of goodness. Oh, gruesome acts are grudging and are in deep grief because of gracious groove of globe that glorifies the goodness at best.

Love is visible when the eyes spark, smile gets and glazes in the face dazzle the aura, gestures get sweetened and lad/less gets speechless as emotions overwhelms throughout their personality. That plays the love of music to give rhythm to life and adore the synchronization of couple or lovebirds who are hitched , mind led with sweet invention ,to cherish the memory of Adom and Eve and reverberates the magical word 'love '. That will dilute humanity favor fibulas procedures of procedures of worthiest world from the patience of goodness, bravery and from the essence of hard toil, sweet and utter dedication to get

Purification of Divine

lesson from the divine power with the statement that eternal love and pure emotions are the powerful tools to let the relations and equalization all above.

Anesthesia is given to make the pain silent that means medication helps the patience to be alive in the dead condition so that operations can be performed to get rid of sickness or deadly disease without many sufferings. So, this medical enzymes boost up the brain to have love and lust for the beautiful life again. Its cons could be weakness, nausea, damage of some tissue or aging. Therefore, opting for the short-cut path may evict and thy life from the beautiful landmarks; sometimes they may be historic one. Hence, be the like the turtles who always preaches to be calm, compose and introvert by power and extrovert by patience who survives quite longer than other creatures because it chose to focus on present so that future sceneries could be fruitful and fantabulas that gives the longitivity and merriness. That always makes them feel longitivity and merriness. That always make them feel youthful, vibrant, versatile, optimistic who sustains in the universe for timeless period by being ageless and also because of their proper diet. Oh! Divine confesses the truth yourself as the bestest creatures who approached in the world with the beautiful reasons to show the power of love, the beauty of deeds and to make the globe gracious yet gilt free.

The each moment of life should be ecstasies, fruitful and full of energy. That makes the person vibrant, versatile and youthful. That helps to clear the hurdles of life with beautiful brain, artistic nature yet full of sophisticated persona. That derives the life to exotica while beautiful dimension is given so as to face the reality of graphing every phases of life elicit, interesting and full of praise.

Deception, villigence, trauma , violence results to ultimate sufferings and where suffocation, pain and grief and grievances all are led down by goodness, beautiful deeds, ultimatum of truth and wisdom that are sheltered under the shed of prodigious pamperness with even exquisite with distinguish jewels of joyful exotica. Oh! I'm in cloud nine where heavens love to fall with Earth and divine dresses in the form of human to cherish humanity to let the social animals understand the power and potential of human body.

The physical human body when understands the equation of chemistry in the air, the biological nature then creates the atmosphere to manifest and mesmerize the globe with tranquil touch of humanity. Eureka, creatures are formed to let the world worthiest with sensible thinking, positive approach and witty brain.

Simplicity, integrity, positive thinking ,honesty when gets the enzymes of passionate desire, complete dedication, then the whole globins strives towards success and human scores the crown of victory ,and divine power blesses the devotees to conquer the world stage to let the deception, betrayal ruin under the feet of love and democracy. Oh! Dedications and devotions are dramatizing the world so much all planets, stars, galaxies, asteroids itself kick the witch and wicked wizards to let the divinity prevail in the whole universe.

Sizzle and smash the cosmos with hard toil, sweat, powerful potential, insane passion to let the human dignity all above. That will conclude to composure, sophistication, innovation, development and growth to grab the underneath potential from the love, blessings and power of almighty. Oh! That's nonesuch achievents where single social creatures love to die for such rewards .Wow, achieving the best from the divinity power to extract my best potential to make the globe glorious yet glamorous.

Stating myself into the position as a heart-throb where every artistic head get startled and perplexed when the dimension and directions of God is followed. The almighty then ultimately power the purest form of love to secure the deadly desire that one can dreamt of. Uh..la..La.. Manifesting my world by breaking the chain of doctorial rules to hoist the flag of democracy. Hummn, human body is breathing in the breathing universe to have a fierce competition with tremendous achievers with whom I'm underdog.

Let's startle the world from the dreary dedication and passionate performance .That will jeopardize all the agonies, sufferings from the power of positivity. The head where positivity is cultivated and the heart from where purity is germinated to realize the power of human body where potential is extracted from the soul. Ultimately, physical body is most powerful tool to mesmerize the world from hard work, dedicated performance to let the dignity get the entity of powerful personality, preaching the lesson to save the naïve and sages and make your heart namby-pamby so that goodness prevails in the human body as divine and absolute with advanced and upgraded technologies.

Cut the crap of nihilism to break the stereotype practices that stereotype practices that's the route of all the junks. That's creeping and crawling all the goodness to greet all the wickedness.

Sun shines with the objectives to scatter light and let the world rocking and sizzling .stars twinkles having the intention to secure brightness by avoiding terror nights. Moon startle the universe with intense tranquility that verves fine atoms to have a positive and peaceful performance. That praises even the tiniest atom to have the romance with the love spreading chemistry from the external as well from the internal world and biological environment too aids to make the scenario of world 'the worthiest one' by adapting the nature of technological instrument and literature section. That will ultimately manifest the world from the assistance of science and science beyond the science. Almighty has created scientists, philosophers, pilots and these tremendous achieved personalities has created the glamorous , glorious and gilt-free world to let the power of education evade all the krypton , cons and riles of life.

Purification of Divine

Immense love is the biggest payment that can't be paid be in the form of monitory value or any physical highest assets that's tangible .therefore, highlight the power, potential, positivity that kill the prejudices to bring prestige in life.

Sometimes, drastic changes transform the scenario of world .The evolution of era and revolutions of the world brings the amenities, sophistications and to make the life happening and simply wow. So, growth and development energies where power and potential of mankind cherishes humanity. Uh….la…la….I'm one of the masterpiece to evade evil and wickedness to fuse the world from the fibulas actions. Oh! Freaks are transforming themselves to be the phenomenal personalities.

Frozen form of glaciers depicts the pictures of transparent life. When it's tortured and hampered by global warming, it melts the tear of emotions which even freeze the deadly hearts of dictators to let the nature shackle free so that beam of sun shines and smile to terrify darkness ,gruesome acts and horror nights. Hummn, earth is getting vanity from the universe to demolish demon hood and over vampires nest to prevail goodness all.

Life is not bed of roses ,it's full if thorns .but when handled beautifully, with attention and care ,it's aromatic fragrance blossoming nature and soft petals creates a beautiful bueguet to come across the walls and bridge to gap of building that's colliding because of discriminations, in equalizations and financial securities, conspiracy that's triggering terrific moments of life slick, easy and tactfully.

Nile river is the longest river in the world that messages to be gentle, have continuous flow, believes in purity and showcase the hidden treasure to dazzle the world to evoke eternal exquisite that life could be full of pleasure and prestige.

A life with full of amenities and physical sophistication can be achieved with beautiful brain, good caliber and insane design and being passionate towards performance ad true love for monitoring values. But when spiritual science is in intact with soul and let the divinity power embraces the beloved devotees with utmost love and utmost care, daring dedication detaches all the hidden treasures that was in the form of killer instinct . Then, almighty showers blessings to make their dream come true in the form of ambition, interest; creative rectifies all the pretty where satisfaction and containment both plays a crucial role to cater best fruitful results.

Statue of liberty has a beautiful message i.e. always stand up for thy rights to show the power and potential for the especially to the women who could be the synonym of liberty, victory and to mesmerize the world from the powerful agenda and to be above all the ridicules things that's hampering them ultimately. That portrays that women are the deities or Goddess who get the entity of sacrifice, beauty, victory, eternal love and an irony at the time of devastation.

Lets cease the catastrophe by catering the chunks of compliancy, standard with tangible luxuries, physical sophistications and invites optimistic thinking with all the possibilities.

Igniting flame in the heart breeds heart core desires into ambition where tremendous achievements are engulfed by the positive aura to secure the best class position in the society. That captures all the attention because of their insane passion and dreary dedication, which puke out the dirt of head to have caliber, sincerity and outstanding performance.

Divine power love to greet their beloved devotees to transform them into the finest creature called 'Human' who love to modify ridicules into rigorous personality where evolution and revolution conjuncts together to preach the definition of real human who are incarnated after crossing the hurdles of eighty-four lacks creature to make the universe as simply out of the world .Hummn, I'm the rising star staying on the Earth to fulfill above the hay still attached with the gravitational force. Oh, yes! Divine powers are conquering the cosmos to let devil sly.

Stepping towards success is the key to unlock all the possibilities and embrace the exotic world from the power of Goddess. Oh! Almighty is creating such a genuine gems to dazzle the world from the sense of education and from the essence of humanity. Yes I'm the one who is bloomed to make the cosmos aromatic.

Sincere commitment and complete dedications always ask for the fruitful result that caters tremendous opportunities to let the frozen head sly from the power of education and intellectual icons. Uh...La...la..., let the world forget to blink from the from the splendid performance of creative panelists to cease all sorts of pain and agonies from the skull of special skilled personality.

Achievements can be grabbed when insane passion and killer instinct fuse together to transform the deformed creatures into intellectual personalities.

Manipulations, conspiracy, hypocrisy, bitching and backstabbers can be eradicated when the positive brain is powerful with sound health. When each brain cells get activated from the absolute power then creative heads like intellects, philosopher, eminent, scholars and bonafied personalities are created to revolutionaries' the world from love, power and dedication towards education.

The lamp of episteme ignites a heart-core desire to secure the ambition world with containment. That also sets real illustrations whatever zeal is abstracted from heart and soul with creative force and craze.

A bond enhances the potential, performance of a person and relations between two parties. Likewise, a bond is when signed between divine and devil in order to conquered the world , threats turns to beautiful treats, opportunities makes the life slick and organization where all organisms are striving hard to nail their performance, proves themselves as bestest

Purification of Divine

creatures to beat the heat of heiniousity to let the cosmos dazzle from the aura of powerful icons. Yaa, victory is proceeding to hoist the flag of crème-de-la-crème in the cosmos. The entire exotica can be elated when noodles nurture their brain with maturity and sensibility ; when heiniousity breeds diplomats to rule the world as giant leaders so as to avoid obstructions, hindrances' in the country. The gentle people occupies and beautiful brain to heat the world as a world as a worthiest planet where all creature love to shelter under divine power and absolute energy. Woah! Human are the bentest creatures to groove the globe with dignity and with complete determinations.

Human, genuine sensible creatures when fused from the labyrinth of hypothetical belief, superstition, dogmatism always calls for conspiracy, confusions, hurdles which ultimately give birth to sufferings, agony, trauma, greediness that vanishes the real charm, goodness and the purity from which he or she is well-known. That also allows hypocrites to believe in dark fantasies, double standard theory and have virtual vision towards life. Therefore, it's good to be real, practical and Greek from the globe of gruesome, hazardous creatures, who grips dirt, devastations, and deceptions to disturb namby-pamby hearts.

People go crazy when fabulous fantasias turns to realities. They observe the scenario of present so as to avoid ill-manner and wrong concept to bring their happiness and project their future at right scale. Then the droplets of award and rewards make the bridge to reach the destination of self-achievements. That's the grace of almighty, the divine power that gives the boon to human to turn as legendary icon and the best sacrament could be aiding to destitute who has nothing but pure blessings and love to make their governor, 'the governor of Nations' in which he/she is highly capable of and the prodigious person grooms with ultimate growth with dignity, pride and with full of prestige of glare to achieve success at par by belong the beloved devotees of divine forces.

Souls are dressed by body shells in which human body shell is the most powerful, beautiful and eye-captivating for all the living creature who strive hard and starve for the treasures that's hidden within so as to drag the world into the state of manifestation. The sizzling performance creates fire in the world stage. That kills heiniousity, bite racy, devastation in the drain that's covered by goodness and creativity of human's potential passion, dedication and tremendous efforts to let the globe Greek about lethargic creatures who sly themselves under the shed of grief grievances, pain, sufferings, confusion that are led down by empty heads, crying for help and even praying the absolute energy to open the gate of mercy, justice, compassion to secure love, adorance and pamper...to greet dignity everywhere.

Fermentation can sometimes give the taste of authenticity... Old wines are illustrious and generally adopted by classy people who get infatuated from intense taste, quality, aroma that it grips on. Therefore, when ethnic taste meets with authenticity, even the gamblers and who juggles with life proceeds to solemn promise to have rewards, achievements in their older ages. As time passes by, that means when time preaches a lot of things , considers as a practical person who grooms in the threats and blooms by acquiring opportunities the most determined as well as the happiest one.

The different phase of life has it's own importance .childhoods considers as the best stage where love is showered from everyone and all the desired dreams will be accomplished by the loved ones. Adolescent teaches to enjoy life with buddies and beautiful butterflies to live the life with full of fragrance in thy orchid. Youth gives a sense of responsibility relationship towards family. At the same time, maturity also aid to build relationship with concerned parties to make their work done, and finally at the adult stage full of pain and sufferings but stills smiles in the face proclaims about that one has throughout his life is incredible and just take sweet synopsis from life to enjoy each phases of life and prove as one of the bestest animals in the planet once you have taken birth. So that world you cherish thy deeds, devotions, dedications at par and considers you as true angels of divine force who approach to conquered the world from the treasures that has extracted from the soul to make the Earth, better place than paradise.

A comma can be a conjunction for a statement that joins two lines to make the statement powerful. Likewise, good action is a conjunction that joins two parties to make the almighty pretty powerful that's hidden within as well as in external world.

Oh God is showering ultimate blessings and grace and boon to their beloved devotees to secure the bestest things that only noodles can dreamt of. Now, let the noodle transform into intellects where dignity head towards the life to open the gate of nirvana. Oh! Divine is awaken to make the fool people the most prestigious yet the powerful one.

When the mood is delight, people opt for amusements and spend leisure period with the loved one to strengthen the bond. Likewise, when achievers are in delight mood that means innovations, drastic development, revolution has taken place to make the globe glorious. Oh devine force are determined to devote energies to extract zeal, passion, hardship from the dead morons and drape the globe from the enchants of slokas, mantras and Om.

The random decisions and haphazard actions always invites chaos and confusion, problems, squabbles and bitterness in relation that are due to lack of sensibility, logics, maturity and the impractical behavior .That breeds violence, hypocrisy , conspiracy, health hazards to make the circumstances catastrophie.Therefore, building the relation stands for making te house'Home' by stretching the bond from love, understanding ,caring and educating the each members to make the planets, the bestest home in the solar community .Dad (sun) is showering spark to sizzle the family from utmost performance sincere commitment and complete dedication.

Let's allow the devine force to each creature and non-living object so that they can balance their relations and existence by coping with each- other .They are related to have good synchronization , mutual concept and sink to make the life beautiful ,fabulous and simply out of the world . oh, abstract form of love when meets person ,even the pricks forgets the feature by gazing the beauty ,goodness ,quality and zeal .Orchid is allowed in aroma ,signifies and the senses beauty of fabuls featuristing floras.

Deceasing someone's potential by underestimating or taking advantage of someone or from bite racy not only hampers someone's status but also destroys their ultimate achievement too. Therefore, it's good to make to hardship that follows sincere dedication that's targets to tremendous achievents. That's getting social to make the life full of harmony.

Health hazards can be the main issues when brain, heart and body system performs the best to breed to verve and ceases traumas and depression. That ultimately greets glamour, grace and goodness to let the dead moron's slying as insects and moths to let the lessions in the cosmos having utmost composure.

Amenities in life make the life slick and sophistication, luxuries greets sophistications. Luxuries greets physical and tangible sophistication to make the human pride of technologies and inventions of the world at the optimum level to adieu dreadful nightmare to secure splendicity at the most superior level.

Dawn comes with vary hues to scatter prestigious, powerful rays of light to avoid terror nights .That always coveys to spark, shine and gleam the cosmos with hardship, dedication, sincere commitment to make the whole tangible and intangible assests physical , biological objects and even the tiniest atom who is deliberated to make the planet and the community happening, love to seize in the sizzling mood to embrace the creativity of protons, neutrons and electrons charged by every single living objects, whose life phrases are determined and controlled to recruite absolute energy once again. Dusk again doctrines about living objects; whose life phrases are determined and controlled to recruit absolute energy once again. Dusk also doctrines about leaving the image in sea, river or pond before shining off the Earth so that world can remember you and cherish and chase your vision and achievements by getting the remarkable legendary lessons. Deeds when determined to refresh and rejuvenate the positive energy, the utmost dedication comes out from the heart core wishes to decease devastation and secure 'Humanism' to create the cosmos , simply ' a prodigious planet.'

Time management plays a crucial role to make the life easy , slick and cosy. Sometimes, a hectic schedule turns the human 'Robot' who knows performance. Sensibility, logics and emotions which are submerged because work is so much worshipped that ultimately human forgets to live their lives and their terms and conditions are also created to abide their emotions and then God sends some seraphs to make the robots realize about Goodness, emotions and feelings. That ultimately transform their body system into loving creatures who also believes in sharing, loving and understanding the concordances, grievances to make their loved ones a beloved. Eureka, gentle love can converts robots to living creatures who believes in heart and angels too.

When oil is greased in robust iron, the machines, the equipments, the equipments or tangible objects begins to work and captivate the attentions from its live performance. Therefore, love , care attention can change the scenes and scenarios of rigorous bones when handled by illustrations icons. They elicit the world from the enzymes of exotic existence.

Team work plays a vital role to bring the efforts of employees at maximum level.That helps to strengthen the bond of collegious and believes in Esperit – De- corps. That allows organizations, institutions, enterprises to meet the desired objectives and grabs goodwill, prestige and fame with all sorts of satisfactions. Hardship, sweat and toil , dedication ,passion and creativity meets their aptitude to bring the amenties, sophestications and luxuries in their lifestyles . That creates tangible source of happiness; and the relations created between the employees brings the sensibility, love, understanding and helping nature. When these two meets together, the organizations turns as home for the employees who approached in te stage to prove themselves a 'Prodigious performer' before the farewell from the 'Earth'. Hummn, divine an deities are buddies to sizzle the performance to let the cosmos ' a place full of composure'.

Let the world get startle from indigenous work that's gripped upon by tremendous achievements legendary icons , prodigious performance whose approach to stick and spark the globe with utmost dedications and become curious personality to make each creature feel a stalk, who rely and get support from their sustainable living and growth. That ignites fire of creativity and also evicts them from their nightmares and dark haunted religions to cease their catastrophe forever. Absolute energies are verving fine thoughts in the well- beings to recruit the universe as authentic religion of seculars stars who are emerged to spread it's nectar to make the sun smile.

The simple person who possess high thinking , even crab- mentality gets hypnotize that add aesthetics in life and helps to produce more personal , to make into world, worthiest. Mahatma Gandhi, a barrister from South Africa when applied his brain to come over from British regime, non- violence movement became a punch for the rulers who were crying to trigger the nation and the citizen from the autocratic dictatorship. They not only capture the liberal head of each people but also seize the happiness, ' Bread and Butter', their family bonding, their breathe 'freedom' without which no single

Purification of Divine

creature can survive. But revolution can take place when the ideology is just confined in detailed plan formulations to execute the action and then India survived to evaluate the world from the epic Indians who are now developed and a signature country, a well reputed in almost all sectors.Hummn, father of India (M.K. Gandhi) was a divine force, incarnated to make the golden bird free from chain, shackles and cage.

A doctor and a medical practitioner always tries hard to prove their work by saving lives. But the case of bucks gives them interest to have luxurious life. No matter, operation or performance is successful or not , but greediness can grudge the person into limited walls , where he/she could not perform the work according to their aptitude, zeal and passion that has nurtured in the form of ambition and satisfaction is not secured which is nerve to lead happy life. Therefore, containment is must. That gives vision through investigation, proper observation to create the scenario as a beautiful accident where beauty meets with feasts to drape the globe with exhilarate power and to shower tranquility all over. Amalgamation in brain makes the skull, full of special skills to have specialization in the profession they pursue. That will ultimately persuade the placidity to have the taste of powerful passionate personalities.

Take a dig , when eminent, researchers and scientists invents for the cause for the leading to development , then their tests and experiments are the approval of their continuous and rigorous efforts who kept the heart and soul to from the outside world, asteroids, galaxies, stars and the other planets and the sun itself .Their formulae , laws, theorem is universally applicable to the related objects that generally concerns about preaching the scientific language and the practical lessons to overcome from superstition or hypothetical world ' These are not adapted easily by the common people and get boycott .But gradually , the brain ideology, modern conceptions, techniques hidden behind the concept, gists proves the world with suitable examples . That permits human to rise in love with approved methodologies and to bereave the humanity at best. Oh , layers of universe is kissing my aura to be cross over the ocean ,earth, horizon and hay and meet the goodness scaling and projecting my deeds to have adorned with divine force.

The laughter gas and the laughter therapy both are contrary to nature. But both have similar significance: they try to make sloths laugh to have proper circulations of blood in the body system, to eliminate stress, tension and depressions in daily course of life, to alive the creature who forgets to live. Beside this, they gives a punch line to life ' Live and let live' and believe in science and trust sciene, beyond the science who gives the theory of prosperous health and in practical, let envy sly within suffering . Therefore, even the Chinese culture adapts and adopts a lot from 'Laughing Buddha' who is symbol of good health, wealth and prosperity. So, in synopsis, it's vivid that thy laugh makes your concerns happy and smile in the face, makes you sensible , witty and intellects who persue to have ultimate laugh in the form of smile from the inner core of heart to abide pain and agony and to reach at the pinnacle of success. Laughing Buddha laughs utterly and Gautam Buddha always had smile in the face that was a sign of witty philosopher and wiser intellects. However, both have vary features. One denotes merry –go-lucky and other hypnotizing successive personalities. Moreover, both gives happiness and keep the person in the state of euphoria .Therefore, laugh and smile rejuvenates the philosophy to have click, sizzling and successful life that smashes the globe to achieve and acquire crème- de- la- crème.

The incarnation of supreme souls are the holy souls when approaches to universe in the form of eminent, genius, saints and sages, philosopher who transform tedious task into terrific achievements that grooves the globe and blossoms human heart from the fragrance of extreme euphoria that may be due to complete dedications, devotional acts, passionate desires and insane hidden treasures that's extracted in the form of fabulas life, iconic personality to stay in the worthiest planet.

The river' Nile ' is the longest and so far the famous hydro house on the Earth. That proclaims about to be progressive energetic, gentle and generous above all, the profounder of gems and skills and enthusiastic about in the lethargic, monotonous life. That not only fascinates the two parties but world also grab the gratifying performance to gratitude the legendary icons and the masterpiece to make the 'Earth' an, exotica.

It's better to define thy personality through the performance that can project the scenario of world at supreme level. That earns biimpas into irony women or the beauty with beautiful brain, who has guts and grip to capture the eyes of sloths and heart of dictators.

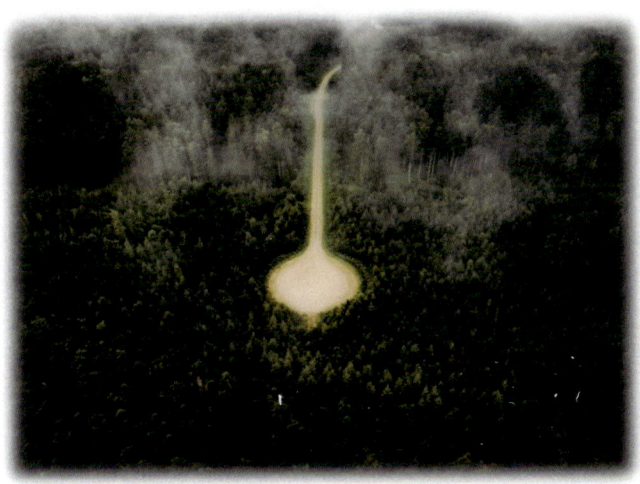

Desert can be moulded into dreamworld when the fountain, the oasis dramatically creates shrubs, plants and living creatures, moths and the life to let the contanation get in touch with eco-system to recruit physical, biological and astronomical surface and surrounding functions simultaneously . That will cocliate the universe from each and every objectives to make the creature and creativity sustain and sizzle. That will gradually smashes the form of work to make the human greek in the term of 'depression', 'devastation' and 'deception'.

A bigwig constituting eternal gems to dazzle the aura and atmosphere in the universe could be the pioneer, panelist, leader, philosopher or the giant icons who has empathy to understand the term to understand the term compassion so that addictions can be involved to bring revolution with endurance. That will revive to positive energy in the world and allow the life cycle to have smooth functions to make the planet 'Earth' , a land of angels.

The diversifications on the world can be brought up by physical, mental, spiritual, biological growth. That brings evolutions, revolution, growth, development to lead the human potential at apex. That dramatically converts age stone era to artificial intelligence era that enequisits the universe from tremendous achievements leading sometimes as a nonesuch existence. The whole world including other planets too loves to pay tribute and credulas to such iconic legends. That leads devastations to mould itself as 'Divinization' where only happiness , containment, development, mutual obligation shelters to absolute energy consisting human body to make the world , the worthiest and the powerful planet. Oh! Divine is verving the virtual pets to evoke their jest of life and understand their existence to have perpetual life and sustainability.

When actions are performed deliberately, then reference doesn't require at all. Their language, hardship, their passion and determination, their aptitude speaks the language of phenomenal performance that triggers all the tragedies and the traumas of life and terrific incidents are created to capture the eyes of backstabbers, bitchy butcher to contribute the almighty, visiting the destinations of good deeds, non-violence, drastic development to eliminate depression, conflicts and conspiracy from the daily course of routine. Oh! Vampires are turning to human to understand the beauty of life, and their motto of existence in the universe to make them extremely energetic, vibecios and versatile.

Amalgamation of thought procedures always brings right decision, correct opinion, and positive perceptions in all dimentions and directions of life. That helps to design, project and forecast the graph of life in the excellent manner and their bright future get directed by the sincere dedication, killer instinct and their extreme and their extreme enthusiasm to modify and manifest the world at the most superior level, to exceed exhilary.

When an exhilary person is full of pain and suffering but still smile in the face always expresses that there is no grievance about about the way of his/her loving. But certainly a message and a lesson can be taken, no matter how hard the situation is , always be a rock- solid mountain so that whoever gaze you , ultimately gets a theme , a lesson and asks about about for the life , that's beautiful. The best reply could be let my passion could live longer than life which will make my name and existence forever to inspire the pupils and icons. Eureka, I am the one turning as masterpiece to make my passion remains more than I exist.

Let's get the enzymes of education to make the ignorant, creeps and crap get rid of suffocations and sufferings. To meet with inventions' and innovations with immense love and caring and passion, education is the life-blood and the basic root to eradicate negative thoughts, depression and conspiracy and hypocrisy. Those will subsequently zeopadise all the hazards and world of sufferings and stick the world to go crazy, worthy and full of liberty.

The cup of coffee energizes you and gives power to be rigorous, passionate and highly determined for the ambition. That automatically boost-up the brain to perform at utmost level and dive the whole world into the ocean of full gems that's oozed from the soul to have cozy life with absolute affirmative achievements. A cup of coffee in the cool café gives all the comforts and cures the cataract, disturbing the life.

Ontology: the study related to nature and being proclaims and preaches to nature and being proclaims and preaches about conservation , care of biological , physical atmosphere surrounding and all the living and non- living objects helps to sustain and support eco-system , living lifestyle to notch-something up for the welfare of world , then the whole divinity power embraces each creature and adore their creativity for the manifestation of mesmerizing globe . This empowers human to distract from blunders, bimbos and bombastic behavior that grudges head to manipulations and conspiracy to make the universe happening and rocking.

    The legacy behind the will exposes the true love for the concerned beloved to secure their financial securities. That makes the ultimatum of the power of attorney that's seized by generous and genuine figure. That abides the terms of bucks and power in the futuristic stage to have a proper and simultaneous growth in the concerned sector that makes them empathy about the ambience of fruits of seasonal sophistication grudging the growth and stashing the secrets of development to have reputed goodwill at the rising level leading to top class faculties . The futuristic planning formulates and executed in the introrary to set the career, the curiosity , the energy and the tempting eyes allures the world to breed surrogacy through the classy panels to have the reputed version of leading the beautiful birth of fantasies , that's nurtured under the arms of their experienced , elegant mentors . Such fantasies' are finished and polished by the beloved to make their action startled and speculated by the whole competition and their rational behavior synthesizes their dream to inculcate in the program me to get executed. That drills all the nasty hacks of life to nail to nudity of performance in the perfect mode so as to frame their immense love and intolerable addiction with the signature of heart- throb and creative catalyst hoisting their flag for undiluted pain that's hidden behind the love to cherish heartiest goal to praise the world at the topmost level.

That teases the dreadfulness to come across and face the breeze and face the breeze of existence encroachments. Then, the density of love will raise the remedy of harshness and the harshness of voice, lead by germs and jerks, brutal having bonds having barbarism to make their beloved existence perceptual and ever- lasting , deceasing the desert of devastating , deception of monsters hidden in the form of concerned relations to make them feeble. Therefore, legacy constituting law generally bears the heroic terms for the person in which he/she is deeply interested in to breach the stereotype pain and practices and follow their Vision that's come in the real estate and extreme enequisits.

The state of anxiety and nervousness both are acts and reacts to build man into human . That gives the sense of responsibility to boost-up for he work performance. Let the anxiety anticipate the brain to make it, strive it, nail it and let the nervousness nurture the tummy so that it turns as terrific shock to transform body system to strive hard and starve, quench and find their aptitude in the beautiful treats and deeds, commanded by their hearts . They will subsidies all the suffocations to serve splendicity That's actually designed to create deliberated mentality hosts to hoist the flag of fortunate fantasies turning out as a refinishing reverie. That's ultimately the epitome of success. Solitaire could be the remedy of jewel lover who're sick to seize secession operation in their body.

Feeding the needy one could be the panacea for the mentality harassed or life threatening person and education could be the best awakening ingredient for the lover success starting personality. That deals with the panacea to overcome from the circle of zeopadise. That also integrates with the approval, evidence and synopsis to notch something up deceasing desertification of life.

The concept in the brain when ambitious then conclusion goes vain. That also scratches synergy and erases the enzymes creating energy bereaving towards chaos and confusion due to disturbance and lack of concentration. That's just because grudging grief and grievances in the head. As a divine blesses and gives boon to their children, then utmost satisfaction is gained. That helps to bring salvation to dig the drain of devastation, drill to nail the potential and performance to recruit the energy and enthusiasm aspiring human to have complete trust and on themselves their zeal and passion , their work will speak the best language , the world love to listen.

The whole world when love to sing the anthem of secularism in chorus, absolute energy verves then almighty spreads the ambience of integrity to inculcate moral values , especially to the social animal' Human' to make the bridge in between the divine and fine human, proceeding towards unique universe . Uh...la...la.. Divine is ancicious to have conservation with human to coverage with itself into the beautiful gift of affirmative energy. Earth, the epitome of successive planet when wants to have connections and conversations with other siblings (planets), ten father(sun) gives extreme blessing to heat the beasts with the beauty , that's generally poured by their children and elderly planets to have a tet- a –tete so as to stun the tiniest asteroids astonished, about the lovely grace, showered by almighty . That permits divine to have perpetual stay in the atom whose main motto is to spread tranquility all over.

Concord when embraces the confined empathy and compassion to sleep and stick the lap of mother nature , condensed cloud creates the circumstances of cloud nine to click the shot and snap of incredible incidents , programmed by human. That steps towards ecstasy and exhilary, doctrines the theory, procedures and methodologies to have enchants of 'OM' in the whole universe, to meet the fortune with fibulas actions to have sense and fence of 'Secularism'. Oh! I am sensing almighty, who etude each being behaviors to forecast functions of body system in the splendid manner to make the moral ethnic and authentic.

The fusion of vary culture i.e. modern, ethnic ,fuddy-duddy, shaggy, sheddy always proves that all beings are equal and sheltered in their unique terms to breed humanity. That synchronizes and elegate the world from the essence of eternal love, mutual obligation, common sense, care and understanding, tranquility so that our sibling gives , is the designation of crème- de- la- crème creature . That also signifies hueful flora of garland, composed together to make beautiful buquet of 'brotherhood'.

Trace the work for the world; fame will eligate your title to entitled thy as a graceful performance. That will beat the heat of heiniousity to have the season of spring in your ever and forever. Buds, flowers, butterflies, colours will cater ambience in the in the orchid to abide pricks that's triggering the purity, generosity, speciality, curiousity of the beloved garland , loved by all the living beings.

Let's alive the moments to cherish the life with extremes beauty hidden within. That will demolish monster and endeavors to elicit y to embrace absolute energy. That will reconstruct the brain of devil to follow divinary forces. Universe will drizzle the purest droplets of tranquility to increase the devotional forces to demolish and fly for high to spread goodness all around.

God preaches their children to perform perfectly, that will ultimately brings pledge, placidity to fascinate thy life. That will build up morale and boost up human power to exclude the frame of felony and furiousity. That allows penance, sacrifice to achieve 'Moksha'. The empire where everything is possible to quench the trust human power to seek containment for the walfare of worthiest creature. This will create the beautiful episodes of tangy,sausy, sweet relations to seek the program, decide by God and Goddess to reach the destinations given by supreme forces. The emotions then evaporated to build the world exceptional.

Luscious fruits of wishes fulfillment can be found from the tress of karma(the beautiful determing deeds) from kalpa- soft,clean and purest heart whose berks could be concerned to actions that allows all the living beings especially social one to step towards supreme knowledge, build the relationship with almighty, delegating affirmative, source of energy to have the victory of divine power.

Ceaseless efforts of work is worship and continuous contemplation of divine force is more than worship or lifeline to encourage and energize freaks , performing felony accompanying the company of creative creatures are must to have smooth ,slick luxurious lives and stating the human into the best programmer. This may result to exceptionally exotic planet where angels are born to have concept of liberal head, heading towards democracy for all the convectional concerned creatures striving hard for the concord universe.

The unique universes when slashes the secrets to have prosperous life, each creature love to cuddle and care from the mother nature that states the world , worthiest where all the living beings are nurtured and nestled in nirvana to build the breeze between beautiful deeds and deadly devastations. The performer(beings) has to decide the path and the directions to lead his/ her life, motto ,ambition where he/she could be freak free from the disasters, taking place in the hypocrite society , also emerge he conspiracy, backstabbing, bitchingness and social violence.

Calamities can be cured from the conservation of forest. Pain can be cured from the panacea given by loved one or supreme energies. Negativity and harshness can be eliminated from peace and work performance that triggers ill-brain and wonderful series of life. That can be jotted doom by the insane dedications, love towards almighty and the evolution and revolution takes place in life.

The spiritual evolution haunts the caliber, captivating the eyes of confined creative panelist to have a crush with ceaseless efforts, whose ultimate destination is revolutions from revilishing personalities that brings out the best potential along with the anticipation of powerful and passionate to prove the world extremely exceptional performance that comes through invocations of almighty and contain completion of the holiest and heartiest energy, serving each creature with immense love to have focus on ambition that has a target to achieve the best in the form of addictive ambitions. That targets to deceiving demons and declaring them to follow fibulas actions proceeding towards divine and deity's destinations.hummn, devoting my love ad the purest energies to embrace permanent pleasures, continuous containment and the heartiest happiness to produce perpetual glory.

Human are best known for their creativities. Some transform them as masterpiece, to allure the universe , their daring dedications, prodigious acts, loveliest therapy, passionate mission are done to manifest the world and mesmerize the universe to beat the heat of heiniusity,taken place due to disturbance, destroyed due to butchers to hamper magical, mystical worship. That captures these Greeks who are diving hard into the ocean of envy.

Historical remarks and legendry icons are the nonesuch landmarks that shows the path of glorious victory preaching the lesions to work hard in the sessions and promising thyself to have glorious destinations . work performance through which target to outstanding destinations, proceeding towards human identity i.e. humanity and proceeding towards fibulas actions i.e. forecasting future at fantasized world.

Fussy heads are the reasons of creating craps, squabbles, conflicts, chaos and confusions who arrive to destroy themselves under the feet of creative skills and specialized heads who are fencing and enhancing their livings their living standard and status, simply out of the world who makes the world go speechless due to external love for their passionate ambitions who knows the language of development ,achievements and arrangements of work sequence and segments. That pleases heart and cleanses brain and splashes live to have a gratitude from the glamour world.

That also raptures all the attentions who also secures salvations stating towards dignified life. With the designation of incredible intellects, born to deceive and diminish the devilry acts, composed by freaky-fussy diplomats, who are distinguished by their democratic behaviors to involve indigenous performers to reckless, ruthless occupations. This not only disturb their relations but also hit their esteem. That insane love meets with utmost performer t rock the world stage in order to ignite flame so as to enjoy the bonfire as celebrations.,,

Eternal love when produced by the emotions and the heart ;the heritage of God then the productivity created by human body directed by creative brain leads to lascivious fruits of karma, also derives deeds to make the social animals as masterpiece who is exceptionally well known for it's beauty. That considerate with purity, brain, and follows actions. Eureka ,a masterpiece; an intellectual icon is invented to make me the worthiest, the versatile and the most creative creatures in the world. Divine is preaching me about the constructive criticism and the true appreciation of 'being human' as [prodigious performer.

Being smart and getting popularity means earning prestige with goodness that traces thy work to every individuals heart so as to kick smirch, sheds behavior and laziness from the body shell. This will help to hypnotize the excellence that in the form of work to be splendid speculations for the passionate panels to judge, inspire and create energetic ,enthusiastic eminent to haunt their real treasures. Eureka, my passion and determination is creating performance at the topmost level to head towards exhilary state.

The incredible infrastructures of the state leads to urbanization where every nook and corners are managed sequentially to have prosperous, luxurious life styles leading to smart city. That also focus on the punch line "the tendency to keep the things in proper order leads to good management".that cuts the crap and smear out the dirt to plunge humanity and hearts of lovely people and bless by superior energy leading to blissful life.

Anticipation in the good deeds deals with fibulas' fortune , incredible work performance and wonderful fate. That always help to empower human to proceed towards ecstasy. That also aid to encourage the needy one to boon and bless them what are really capable of and what they desired of . that helps to fulfils not only the needs of deprived one but also help the person to achieve the most satisfying objectives in their interested zone to settle squabble, conspiracy, back-bitting,bitching the man to be the sufferer.

Hormonal imbalance in the human body leads to several diseases, sufferings changes to mental and physical behavior. That breaches the delicate bonds concerned to hyper stress, dictatorial rule, destructive criticism, depression and traumas led down by drastic changes in genes and chromosomes. therefore, proper balance diet ,adequate water, physical exercise, meditations devotion of Gods and determination towards work always results in balanced life with mature thinking, brotherhood feeling to be freaky in the gruesome world.

Ancient sages and saints has the power to cure all the health hazards through the enchants of slokas and mantras, yoga and meditation, ayurveda and some perplexing phenomenon which are hard nut to crack. The power of positivity also makes all the assignments up –to the mark and special skills are adopted and adapted by the skull to secure peace and the sprouts of knowledge to have lip-smacking fruits of creative performance.uh..la..la.God is having glance to their children who are fascinated to tempt the world with glory, development and achievements.

Haphazard action sometime leads to problematic issues. That are caused by crude decisions whose feedback or results are not considered at all. That chucks the organizations especially the top level managers to face extreme hazards and enormous difficulties which can wrap up the organization. enterprise, institutions because of lack of adequate knowledge, unity, proper synchronization, positive attitude, mutual understanding and co-operation. That leads to disturbance that has to be diagnosed from the advisory board, to deliberate the assignments, formulate plans and policies in the realistic approach to abide clumsiness.

Transformation of stone age era to technological era depicts that social animals co oversized into the bestest creatures " human" that can be entitled as seraphs born to eliminate the lamp of light , getting rid of horror nights and darkness. the human intelligence when cope-up the artificial intelligence, the whole universe gets overwhelmed by twinkling stars, composed moon, gracious galaxies, astonishing asteroids to make the entire solar system step towards supreme power to smash exhilarations on divine force are emerged to hypnotized the world from love with liberal heads, happiness wit holiest approach and development with designed destiny. The sense of secularism and the bonding of brotherhood is blended to get unique universe.

Purification of Divine

The spiritual grow th of person makes his/ her persona powerful. That allows the spring season to pour rain to rejuvenate life, revive energy and enthusiasm to stick and stash splendidly. That verves positive energy, confidence is gained and the brain is occupying beautiful creative networking with emotional heart, then an individual converts into prodigious performer, whose personalities are boost up by the antique treasures to make the cosmos elegant.

The petals of flowers are namby-pamby by nature. Their tender feature depicts that one has to be flexible, sensitive, versatile and should have the goodness to move the hears of people. Their aroma, their charm teaches to spread fragrance in the world in the form of fibulas work, beautiful creations, philanthropic actions and devotions to God that are loved, pampered and adored by each creatures. The holy home; heritage of divine is the deepest area of heart, hymning the song of love and beauty to add aesthetics in body shells to place enormous possibilities.

The methodology of creating connections and communications with people to make the life slick, easy, strengthening bonds, who enraptures with positivity and special techniques to change the perceptions of clumsy people, crab-mentalities who suffers from negative thinking, trauma or depressions. that also embellishes the life with dignity, charm, beauty to enhance the elegance worn by human with well- known designations with distinctive achievements . oh! Divines are embracing me for the love that is showered in the form of awakening lazy bones and evoking sloths to secure the spark so as to let the world sizzled.

'Om' is the word that is loved, spoken and enchanted even by the almighty, supreme force, the absolute divine, God and human who feel they're true devotees of absolute energetic power. The complete sentence 'om' doctrines about the concord cosmos, come to conquer and capture complete universe for the amalgamation of assets that's hampering because of agony, suffocations and crude thoughts. The most powerful term is slick, smooth and has the power to set staircase to proceed paradise oh! An exclamation and Om is everything, the cutest curve of crème- de- la- crème.

The supreme sublime energies releases the absolute love towards the work that thy perform as worship. That oozes the eternal passion to enhances the creativity to let the special skilled skull get the enzymes of artistic caliber to surpass pain, caused by bitchingness and loatheness.

The agenda to provoke inner conscience brings the most creative treasures that was elevating the brain to enshrine the world in the form of special talent that are empowering the power house of cerebellum, cerebrum and modulo oblongata. The shock converts to terrific moments of life the whole skull in charged with creative skills and absolute power to scatter positive atoms in the body system to bring out, best in the human potentials so as to startle their world with dignified designations.

The creamy clouds when presents seven sizzling colors in the form of rainbow, the world smiles the world smiles with the colorful creature to spread the hue of beauty, eternity, positivity, splendidly that triggers all the pain and suffocations to let the world' worthiest'. Yes, I am adorable creature in the worthiest world who come with the intention to spread immense love.

Almighty when embraces their beloved devotees to secure seat in his/her lap, the nature showers infinite blessings and tremendous opportunities to blossom their world completely and spread ambience of euphoria to mould the wicked, witch and wizards into worthy, vibesious personalities.

Divine force are the pure energies that creates bonafide people to manifest the world. Their passion, actions, determinations enthusiasm verves the fine thoughts in the individuals to make the life enthusiastic, energetic and pretty optimistic. That makes the planet-earth, exotica.

The word, 'beauty'' is beyond to describe. It's the pure eternal feelings that spread ambience in the heart that caters fragrance to mesmerize each individuals from human deeds, their phenomenal actions, their pure conscience, , optimistic behavior, positive approach towards the life to make simple things to make simple lfe outrageous and extraordinary. Loyal and royal destinations entitling the distinct destinations. Oh ! beauty is sticked to victory to secure endeavor achievements to make lives simply wow.

God is the ultimate force to elongate human life in the bestest way to love goodness to transform heinous and noodles into tremendous achievers to shelter nirvana in each human hearts to Perform for tranquility, in order to conquer the world with dignity, self-esteem and with good reputations. That will cease all the catastrophe to cater concordances all around That leads creativity to the eyes of brilliant comments who are incarnated to spark, shine and tranquil the world.

Devine and deity doctrines about the developed skills that drizzles absolute verves to groove the universes gloriously and graciously. that ultimately drapes the cosmos into the closet of concordances that caters cosyness, charm, creativity. That gradually elevate and inexquisit the persona of living beings especially human to be bonefide, brilliant and best in their area to give gratitude and tribute to supreme energies. Yes, I a am a masterpiece who is born to replicate the Paleozoic era, the most powerful yet placid era where irony is magnetic personalities to head the held high.

Sun's bacon when scatters light, aura of every creatures shine and spark to let the world glow gloriously, especially the human who believe in holiness, their aura speaks goodness, that makes iconic and Immensely powerful. Sages and saints always perform penance, devotiontional deeds and invest their time in curing pain, suffocations and prepares remedy for mental upliftments, through speech , natural therapy, enchants of mantras and slokas. That dominates devastations and favor fabulasly.that praises actions and power led by almighty itself.

The heroic actions when performed by heart throb, fan followers salute them for their phenomenal job that's done completely by their hearts that is linked with brain to believe in the tremendous achievements conferred by enormous love and complete dedications for their insane passion to cherish ' humanism', that only understands the language of goodness, justice, compassions beautiful actions, philanthropically works, development, dignified life and speaks the language of holiness, purity, moral value to pay tribute to divine force, supreme energies and almighty.

Beauty benefits the heart and set of classy standard to enhance the aesthetics of life. God- the supreme energies blesses their devotees to design decorative paths to have loyal destinations where royalmasts exists. Beauty enexqiusit living beings to pursue the empire of enormous possibilities leading to masterpiece having powerful monarchy.

Marching for the mesmerizing destinations, always allow human associations to persuade the devilry power through contained contemplations, powerful , powerful presentations, distinguished destinations, suspicious speech, vivid visions for objectives and clear concepts towards definite goals leading to splendidly and phenomenal performance top achieve sacred space in almighty's lap.

Each cell and every atoms of human body when turns vibrant, energetic and absolute, a masterpiece takes birth to rejuvenate the universes with most powerful mantra 'Om' that detoxifies all the negativities, depression, anxieties to drain conspiracy, hypocrisy, back- biting. That allows human to form actions to proceed palatial destinations.

Destinations are the eventual point that design beautiful destiny of human through absolute divine force to trace terrific movements of life. That's jotted by tremendous efforts and excellent performance. That uplifts social standard to seize sarcasm from the daily hectic routine.

Divine is the powerful source to make human understand about the absolute affirmative approach that revives happiness, prosperity, growth, sophestications and preaches to perform philanthropic actions, have the sense of compassion, and justice to have contained life.

The absolute energy and the supreme power has the objectives to perform the best and stash the scret of splendid senero to have secred cosmos. That generally focus to fascilitate the world with fabulas actions and tremendous achievements. The whole world then startle to have visualizations of almighty's incredible actions who are incarnated to spread tranquility ,, splendicity, from the beautiful creativity to make the planet peaceful yet phenomenal.

The ancient mythology and the holiness of pure energies when integrate together, then Bible, Kuraan,Gita,Aagam preaches about the purity that's linked with the heart- the heritage of the God and the shrine of simplicity and humbleness. That symbolizes about the splendid world who is ready to embrace exhilaration and seizes sin because of exceptional penance that's showered in the form of ambrosia to cut the crap of catastrophe. That helps to eradicate felony by elaborating the concept of devotion, dedications and deeds and to endanger elatedness. That also enexquisit all the eras to have happy, hillerious life away from heinous world.

Transformation of women and men to human is possible through devotion of good and dedications towards philanthropic action. That always design the destiny to distinguish destinations, that eradicates felony to greet the glorious globe and to have prosperous, luxurious life.

Onametophia is the term that's relate to 'tick-tack', 'ring0ring', a kind of phrase that generally emphasis on beautiful sound coming out to tranquil the brain and evoke the body system in order to give rhythm to the hearts and becomes the beautiful lyrics to smoothen eardrums and lips as a fabulas actions, the whole universe then shower serenity over the sensational seraph to make every beings love eternity. Wow! Wicked wizards are now sheltered to shed their evil and transform them as devotional devotees. Wow, the worthiest world is simply out of the world.

Divine and deities are the positive force who sparks individual's life and transform them to incredible life where she/he gets utmost blessings and serenity from the tremendous efforts. Hardship, dedications to modify the scenario of the world to overwhelm humanity.oh! well-beings are healing the sarcasm to spread the essence of exotic world.

Absolute energies are pretty affirmative who detaches problems to have the best possible solutions. That eradicates barbarisms and superstition. That preaches about the beauty of devotional deeds and dedication towards the job assignments that always proceed towards ecstasy.

Life is full of energy and verve when peace pursue the destination of perfection and elites embraces the exhilaration to follow freedom, shatter the shackle of solitudeness to invite intelligence , integrity and independence to let the condemn heart get burst of from the bubbles of overwhelming emotions.

That helps to remove all the obstacles of life through the enzymes of ethics , etiquettes and education, inspiring each individual to be intellect and have indigenous performance to relax in the bosom of beautiful cosmos.

Mother nature smiles when sensational solar families bless and grace the planet 'Earth'' to be the epitome of perfection where all living and non- living creatures carve their destiny of incredible intellects to be vibecious, worthiest and versatile who solely trust in the theme 'esperit- de= corps' to make the prestigious planet into the state of crème- de-la-crème.oh! condensed clouds is pouring emotions to each beings to settle them in cloud nine.

Almighty astonishes when every beings turn beautiful to make the world, breathtaking. Supreme energies then shower serenity and mould seraph to make the world worthiest and every moveable energies and each atoms ,molecules suppress pain to secure splendicity.heartfelt invocations always invite God to have he taste of love and emotions that is presented In the form of devotions, prayers, secraments, exceptionally beautiful deeds to credulous the universe that's beyond to describe.

Perpetual penance of coal transform the resource into dazzling diamond which is precious, priceless and prodigious. That simple piece of charcoal convert themselves ass masterpiece and preaches the lessons to be the perfectionist. This has come to set an historic landmark to make the entire corporation perplexed. The whole world then gratitude the masterpiece for nonesuch actions whose hard toil sacrifice, daring dedication, devotional activities, pump the hearts of gem juries, with rejuivience and the enthusiasm to focus on the passion that has inculcated in the form of ambition. Therefore, supreme energy force cleanses our heart to love almighty and blesses their devotees to be the angels whose main objective is to magnify and manifest the universe with minute detailing perusing perfection. Diamond is dazzling ambrosia to make their ancestors, collegous and their future generations to make the lives exceptionally unique and set the instance of legendary icons.

Divine embraces devotees to be scumpicious, sensational and simply out of the world who are incarnated to work incredibly nonesuch to tribute the supreme force from their tremendous achievements, terrific performance , prodigious assignments to make the entire get the taste of integrity, authenticity and moral values to sizzle absolute energies., bonafied to rock the world and sizzle every individual hearts from their beauty, creativity, actions, determinations, passion , caliber to design concord cosmos.

Transformation of tedious tasks to terrific assignments grooves the globe for better upliftments. That changes the scenario of world to drizzle the droplets of determination, passion and sensation to have palatial destination proceeding towards loyal and royal success. The journey from caterpillar to butterfly always teaches to modify thy actions for the betterment of world and for the sake of humanity that always proclaims to be best for all the living beings and entitle them to be crème- de= la crème.

Cosyness and concordances always integrate together to make the human pretty powerful who embraces elite world to secure victorious villae.that always lead to democratic vision cherishing ' freedom' in order for better lifestyles, their work performance which also shows their attitude, aptitude and aesthetics for their beautiful brain that's exhibited in the form of creativity, positivity, integrity and specialty. That enexiqusit holy shrines- heart to manifest the world with utmost dedication, insane passion and tremendous achievements to smash and sizzle the cosmos for the continuous concatenation.

Divine force blesses their devotees to achieve the best and groom, bloom and croon the cosmos to have peaceful planet where they are interested to stay in the bosom of mother nature to mesmerize the master piece's destiny. Almighty then help supreme energies to create absolute force to make the universe extremely astonishing where all the living beings believes in the theory of drastic development, enormous growth, smashing seeds to make the world feel credulous for their nonesuch actions.

Absolute energies verves [positive approach especially in the human life that always teaches to more ahead in life and extract the best potential and passion that's hidden in the heart to carve the creativities in order to be worthiest treasure. That will not only makes the person prodigious but also grooves the globe gloriously and graciously to have dignified life with distinct destinations. Eureka! I am an incredible icon and who solely trust on indigenous actions and exceptional performance to enhance the life-style of artists, lovers, leaders, philosophers and intellects to enjoy in the beautiful encroachments.

Devine and deities are the supreme force that accompany with absolute energy to create masterpiece legendary icons. Historic personalities who believes in nonsuch actions and pay tribute to the entire globe by their heartfelt emotions that can be depicted in the form of credulous, catering creativity y=to achieve the acquaintance of devotion, dedication and diligence. That drapes and design the cosmos closet with the emulsion of eternity, integrity and authenticity.

Let's enjoy the scumpicious life in the bosom of mother nature that generally allows all the well-beings to love the beauty of biological environment whose mystical worship create miracles to rhe nature lovers. Oh! Breath taking sceneries are allowing me to have smooth breathtaking process. Oh! Paradise exhales..

The definitions of life is to achieve the best, secure splendicity and spread serenity to surround all the well beings in the cozy atmosphere where beauty is the core concept of heart and duty is the foremost requirements of individual and creativity is the most crucial to let the universe sustain smoothly. That will cater chunks of be wilderness to make the world wonderful.

Devine power also help their devotees to believe in goodness and have trust on themselves. They convert noodles into witty intellects. Person's physical, psychological, spiritual growth and evaluation

Boost up their morale, confidence, diligence, energy, enthusiasm to make the whole universe pretty powerful who always prefer to sing the anthem of drastic development from Devine force in order to gratitude almighty.

The supreme energies when preaches about supreme knowledge concerning to creating masterpiece, catering piece, carving God made sculptures to enhance enequisits on earth and communicating with absolute force to project and forecast the whole life of thyself as well as the entire community believing in goodness and philanthropic actions to create the cosmos full of creative head composure, concord to have smooth confiscation by almighty.

Devine drizzles diligence to design the devotees into magnificent manner. That also carves their creativity to get the designation of masterpiece. That helps to décor human life with essence of euphoria and with the sense of achievements. That replenish the world beautifully to rejuvenate living beings especially human to perplex the placidity with powerful presentations, prodigious performance and prompt actions. That transforms scenario of the world d to make each individual incredibly iconic and simply out of the world.

Dressing the delicacies decors and enhances the beauty and taste to fall in love with lip smacking food. That allows the senses to enjoy the auspicious world where love, emotions, harmony integrate together to smash the world from the freshness and fragrance of beautiful bouquet symbolizing secularism. That empowers divine forces to defeat evil and wicket wizards to entertain in the encroachment of euphoria , where supreme power succeed. Oh! Powerful preachers are perplexed by their kids who are kind, compassionate , supremely powerful and exceptional to transform, especially the human life at a grand scale. That creates palatial destination designed bee divine and deities, to drizzle diligence ,devotion, dedication for the deeds and dedications of work to be blessed, blissful and beautiful life. Devine, deities, God, almighty and supreme force energizes to verve enthusiasm to define the universe- the place full of educationalists, full of eminent encouraging and empowering to divinity to drape the beauty, creativity, sensibility, integrity, authenticity to have the security of cozy, concord cosmos : driving the term divine succeeds and achieve historical success to be the candid of supreme force- the absolute energy.hummn divine is having the lascivious fruits of divinity to be in the distinct positions.

Divine, supreme energy, almighty,pure powers always proves their devotees as creme de la creme.They send their beloved kids to secure highest ranks in all the universes by their deeds,love, good jobs and by their insane determinations. Beloved devotees of all such supreme force not only to rule all the universe but also to present all beautiful gifts to divine in order to mesmerize them,cherish them and evoke them and realize them that their love for me and such Incredible personalities are always true. They also give solemn promise to themselves that they will head their held high to make their pure powers insaperable as long the soul and core of almighty sustains.

All the eras and time get astonished and pleased when the miraculous journey of any incarnated personalities are born as they bring absolute revolutions and rejuvenate them for their successions.oh! I am the one who is succeeded to make the time and eras and their concerns more fabulous, powerful and utterly advance.

Beauty in the eyes,happiness in the heart, smile in the lips and asthetics in the soul bring exotica in the living beings that cherishes success, money, power,fame, love to bring achievements.with highest remarks and makes the human to realize the eternal love that proceeds to nirvana.Wow! I am adoring in the loveliest portion of the world to enequisit myself from the scrumptious fruits of good karmas.

Genes, harmones, heredities help human to extract creme de la creme from the potential, passion and persue prodigious professions, have proud not only to parents but also divine energies who wish to see exotic world, better than ever. Wow I have extracted the best genes from the parents to make the supreme power fabulous . Above all, this can be synopsis that seeds of papaya will give birth to papaya plants. Seeds of greater potential couple give birth to iconic personality. Extract the best genes and heredity babies in the womb to conquer and rule in the World.

Nature when mesmerizes with breathtaking beauties,sky overwhelmes with joy,dew drizzles, glaciers turns golden due to sun' s bacon, hills feels amazingly strong though the fountain showers acqua with the music of symphony. Wow, our planet is cosiest.Devine, supreme force,pure energies love to stay in worthiest world and they're sheltering to make this world, nirvana.

Let's ignite and illuminate the planets with karmas, actions, passion, love and with eternal beauty so that they can transform ourselves as obeisance to the God.yes catastrophe happens, disaster takes place, accident causes and hurt humanities but beauty can be implemented by planting more trees, being safe and awaken from all the hazards to escape all the jeopardize situations of the life and add spark to bloom as lotus in the ditch. Even deities and divine enjoys in that purified seat, that's lovely, beautiful and above all, like deserts in the oasis.

Absolute divine power dresses the aura magnificently and allow them to shine as twinkling stars that gets praises, pride and popularity to mesmerize the earth with aroma of ambrosia that has extracted form of passionate performance ,insane creativity that has flowed from the ink of eternal love emotions ,peace from the heritage called 'heart'.

Theme based on peace cause for love, secularism, brotherhood, education, generosity. that binds the earth into tolerance, common sense to bring unity and revolution and evolution of era to create golden phase jotted by valuable time to manifest the earth leaving no stone unturned..'

Uniform performances when blends with utmost dedications and sincere commitments, incredible results to revolutionaries the earth with the genes of eminent, global leaders, intellectual icons who are the main roots of prestigious planet 'Earth', come to cater the value of education in order to transform the social animals into best and beautiful creatures on earth who are entitled as "human".

We are in the twenty-first century, in a new millennium which has crossed all the hurdles from esazoic era to pelazoic era to beautify the senerio of the world by converting devastation into splendid destinations so as to rock the stage with humanity, having the shells of education and shield of love, generosity, nobility, tranquility, justice to get the victory over manipulations, conspiracy. Trauma techniques and wicked and sin acts. Oh gosh! I am in the best stage of human life, creating the beautiful episodes to lead the world from he power ,potential, passion to get the degree of self-achievements.um..saluting almighty as the world started saluting me.

Let's take an assumption; paper sheets when goes in the hands an artist, he/she draws beautiful painting and goes into art galleries, it captures all the attention of paintings

Loves as it contains the hidden meanings and outer concept that seizes visitors attention to get praise and price. That ultimately jot down destiny of artist into the bestest way. That's the power of adorance, compassion and passion that rectify all the amendments of life to bestow his/her life from the indigenous, insane performance called the true love for her/his work.

Charcoal is black in color. That's infect the color of power. It detoxifies all the dirt and impurities from the skin and diminishes melanin that makes the outer shell 'skin' soft, supple and radical free. so, the synopsis is to get rid of stiffness, rigidness, and dirty brain compressing with pain, conflicts, squabbles and start believing in goodness that's the real beauty infect coming out from the pores of purity. Goodness, eternal love, and the blessings of almighty.

Special performance infect add gleam, spark in the work and genuine love ,passion and insane creativity when stirs together , that gives splendid affect to design the assignments authentically artistic. Intrinsic love for the work performance gives the signature of dignified , designation holder called 'seraph 'born on earth to décor the planet with purity, tranquility and insane creativity.

Sweepers clean the roads in order to make the sanitations clean and trees are planted to maintain greenery in the surrounding so as to balance eco-system and maintain hygiene at best. That caters opportunities for the biological environment to get the chemistry of love from the physical and tangible assets. Likewise , when the physical bodies is detoxified with pure things such as aqua , milk, yogurt, curd, fruits and all the essential nutrition than human body, machines, skull gets the nourishments of healthy, hygienic and nutritious food that allows the human to stay fit and when brain is cultivated with positive thinking ,life ultimately gets positive attitude to secure anything what one has desired of . Therefore, cleansing of brain and body purifies the soul and heart. That ultimately tempts heart to secure purity ,generosity, nobility, cleanses skull skillfully and dazzle the enzymes positivity. That ultimately drags the person into the fountain of elatedness where humanity oozes and the bubbles of brotherhood shelters the hard rock heinous world to transform them into heavenly cosmos. Oh! Almighty grace their devotees...

Moon live to see the great wall of china , that's exceptional example of the architects who came on the earth to seize the attention of solar family. Ah! That's a tremendous achievement infact. Love to conquer the world from my achievements now, so that I get salute from the shining stars who are even the synonyms off tranquility. My synonyms is victory.

The castle of love can be created when manipulation, ego, beachiiness, psychological tortures' are to be buried under the submerged wall so that concrete path of exotic destination eligate the beautiful castle of magnificently.

Let's make even the tiniest atom positive so that brain and body gets the absolute energy where divine meets with the body mechanism to spread the enzymes of purity and positivity and makes the human utterly powerful who has the passion to conquer the cosmos from hard determinations, passion,, enthusiasm so as to dilute the earth as a worthiest planet where each and every phylum connects with eco- system so as to make the human utterly powerful and the best creature in the planet. Hummn... getting vibecious , versatile and leading into the path of achievement.

Birds chirper when nature embraced them and allow them to nestle in between the green woods to spread melody all around. That alive dead morons to gaze the globe and glorify them with true spirit, killer instinct and passion proceeding towards perfections.

Amalgamation of thinking invites positive thinking and procures placidity where new brain cells emegered to detoxify the whole body that submerges all the negative energies to transform social animals into human where they can anticipate into world class deeds to achieve their ambitions best and polish their performance to perfection.

Philanthropy works as an excise duty to the person who believes in being human and the power of attorney is in the hand of almighty , divine forces as well as in human itself.

Human bodies consist of powerful elements which can break all the shackles of stereotype mentality to mesmerize the world with dignity, good designations to defeat the world's disaster raised due to nasty acts and dictatorship[.

Work resistance and tremendous efforts on performances polish the potentials to addict the passion .this will gradually extract precious pearl from the shell that are submerged beneath the sea, who comes in the handle of gentle to make the heinous and noodle calm, compose, intellectual, to believe in the goods. That's infect a kind of therapy to reduce frustrations and furiousness and also meditations powerful gem to detoxify negative energy especially from the brain to be a chilled out person. Therefore, work when conducted with absolute source and positive energy, skull and whole skeleton gets specialized skills for the splendid functions of inner world and the outer one. that simultaneously smoothen the scenario of elicit world.

Holistic heritages and pilgrim centers consists of deeply magnetic forces that induces positive vibes , absolute atmosphere and affirmative energies. Gorgeous hearts, devotional people, religious groups gets tempted and love of divine forces to make them bestest, lovliest and the most beautiful creatures of the universe. Oh.,my-my..! speechless to describe the outburst emotions that's overwhelming all around.oh! I am a peaceful soul spreading serenity to surpass devastations because of which humanity is dying under the regime of dictators.

Let's bury the hatchets to blossom the world at par. That'll cater fragrance of love, compassion justice and bind the hueful floras to make the beautiful bouquet of brotherhood and secularism so that sun, its members, stars, galaxies and asteroids feel fabulous and ambiguous to let the earth rock from its revisiting recruitments and fabulous features.

Strategies of life must be formulated and should be implemented so that people extract their best zeal to achieve ambition so as to modify the sceneries of world with their brain power , positivity and super skills that makes the whole globe proud, glorious and simply out of the world.

The world is mushrooming as sky rocket who is killing themselves to touch the pinnacle of success, who also adore and admire the hay where there is infinite scope of succession, achievement and complete freedom.

The fierce competition from a person itself is nonesuch. That ultimately targets to legendary personality where the life is encyclopedia initiates of the term 'success', If-achievements. that warmly welcomes insane passion, incredible creativity, utmost dedications to bring revolutions in the world to evoke dead morons and lazy literates about the power of tremendous efforts and purity of heart that's enveloped and attached with souls.

Architects design the mansions with the objectives to create heavenly home ,where family members enjoy together, get relaxation and sophestications where vibes are absolutely positive cosy and full of divine energies which can only get entry with love in the heart and smile in the face. That's the beauty of creating bond with the members and goodness of heart to create good communications with them. That makes mansion vibecious , versatile and verdicts to victory's villa whose single soil gets fame , recognitions and popularity to catch all the attentions of the dwellers as well as the jewelers.

Concrete path tells the tale of hard toil that's applied with tremendous efforts, tedious yet terrific journey. That teaches the beauty of devotional patchy work that's performed with complete dedications and distinguish feature. that Detroit portions to convert them to slick, strong roads. Likewise, hard toils bewilders the eyes of ignorant and frozen brains who are dying and slaving under the deadly dangerous animals called dictators, who mercily kills their own dynasty, because of autocratic, barbaric mentality feels exciting and anxious to seize

Others job by letting others feel pathetic, breaking the chain of love, ultimately slues their dynasty. Therefore, positive attitude with eternal love combines together, liberalization is followed. under the democratic vision which believe in the theory of 'live and let live' and trust on the concept, detailed by the idiom 'now or never'. that gives fruitful result to believe in yourself, good deeds and be generous to the needy one. That should be the agenda of secular as well as liberal world to make the globe glorious and glamorous.

Grief and grievances breaks the potential and relation of people but positive approach proves the person the bastes creature arrive in the universe to show the power of education, passion to create the world into the worthiest place and penance for the job performance to rock the world stage with self-esteem dignity and to get desired course of actions to let the cosmos ignite the flame of benefice personalities, ideal icons and eminent where development, innovations, revolutions are main gist of planet called 'Earth'. So , let's grip the grief in such a way so that tectonic threats turns into beautiful treats and groove the globe in glorious way where single gaze can modify the age stone era to artificial intelligence developed era.oh! love pollution in the brain, heart, individual and biological environment is dominating peace.

Peace is a quench that every single creature love to get and it's basic rights to live the life with peace and dignity. That evaluates the person to jot his/her career at a high scale. That makes the graph off life slick , sound and superb, simply out of thee world. As calm and compose mind relaxes the nervous system and greets fellowship[and courageous to stay in unity, believe in the positivity and achieve the ambition that targets to evoke social animals called human' that they're the best living things that supreme divine power has created. Yes, serenity is utmost need that everyone must have to decompose pain and devastations and to bury all the hatchets, that's leading towards sarcasm, aggression and polluted heads.

Latest innovations and inventions that has proved that globe is leading towards advancements that has even made good connections with other planets so that living creatures seek assistance from their buddy planets at the time when needed.wow! we're in the new millennium , 21st century is smashing and sizzling the cosmos to perform every single individual in to way of 'crème-de-la-crème'.ahh! human are contained with satisfactions. When protons, neutrons, electrons integrate together, positively charged particles, negatively charged particles combines together that produces heat, that also cause reflections to produce nuclear energy. To prevent nuclear energy from all the possible hazards, rice bran and leaf manure create compost manure to safeguard nuclear energy. Eureka, Scientist and Novelist are designing the universe as the epitome of perfection. Oh my ...my ..the series continues..

All the atoms, protons, neutrons, electrons integrate together in large volume for the formulation of atomic mass. Oh Yaa, in this methadology, nuclear energy is produced. Divines in the form of astronaut and scientist are revilishing the entire solar communities, stars, moon, galaxies and milky way.

Purification of Divine

God has created human and human invented developed gadgets. When human and gadgets collide together, nature gleams as spark of human becomes specialized to describe their potential and gadgets become healthy and source of wealth to describe the unlimited power of human and God smiles with the love to see them synchronize that's leading the planet to be the perfect epitome of paradise.serinity… we are proceeding to show the agenda of love towards each living and non- living things to breed the eternal euphoria. Now, the jug is full of junks.

The backdrop portion plays a crucial role to sizzle the performance and catch the attention of audience. That add grace into the show and to justify the artistic concept of the show that proclaims, opinion and mentality of the whole show, the co-ordination and the theme for which the performer is loving to sly herself/himself to diagnose their zeal and passion so that they can earn well and reach the ladder of success. Therefore, external backdrop help to show the internal stage of the performer so that their ambition or heir main theme can be portrayed to let the world mesmerized. Yes, love the peace within that I secure from which I ignite fire to call me a legend, who is deprived with virtual payments" conspiracy"- the gambler plays to disconnect others for their personal benefit. Still happy, contained and adore the policy of placidity that has given birth to angels to spread serenity all around, especially to the home called 'earth'.

The heritages, pure destinations, temples, shrines, churches, mosques ,monasteries, archeologolic elements , magnificent mysteries are full of magic and miracles especially when are situated beneath the earth in the natural forms. They are insanely powerful and beloved. They aspire their devotees to create eureka moments in all aspects of their lives and accomplish all the wishes and desires anyone can ever imagine of ....They are out of the world as they are beyond and beneath our planet' Earth', emerged according to their will .Wallah .. I am blessed to get loved from such Out of the world pure destinations who jotted prec destiny .

The equator of the globe classifies the poles and regions named as: east, west, north, south. That also gives emphasis to seven continents and four coastal seas. That derives about the global matters, their pros and cons, modifications required for the betterment and up gradation of the world , cosmos fascination i.e. the superior graph of the earth to tempt other planets(on the basis of humanity, generosity, brain power, human potential, true dedication on job performance and devotion towards supreme energies, innovations and drastic development on technologies etc) to spread the splendid scent on sphere: globe. Oh

Purification of Divine

yaa, quench and striving hard and starving with tranquility to transform purification of divine... purification of divine... purification of divine....

www.ingramcontent.com/pod-product-compliance
Lightning Source LLC
LaVergne TN
LVRC090441090526
838199LV00117B/541